The Bible from Scratch

Available in the Bible from Scratch Series

The Bible from Scratch: The Old Testament for Beginners
Genesis from Scratch: The Old Testament for Beginners
Exodus from Scratch: The Old Testament for Beginners
The Bible from Scratch: The New Testament for Beginners
Matthew's Gospel from Scratch: The New Testament for Beginners
Mark's Gospel from Scratch: The New Testament for Beginners
Luke's Gospel from Scratch: The New Testament for Beginners

The Bible from Scratch

The New Testament for Beginners

Donald L. Griggs

WJK WESTMINSTER JOHN KNOX PRESS
LOUISVILLE • KENTUCKY

First edition
Published by Westminster John Knox Press
Louisville, Kentucky

13 14 15 16 17 18 19 20—20 19 18 17 16 15 14 13 12

Book design by Teri Vinson
Cover design by Dilu Nicholas

Library of Congress Cataloging-in-Publication Data

Griggs, Donald L.
The Bible from scratch : the New Testament for beginners / Donald L. Griggs.
p. cm.
Includes bibliographical references.
ISBN-13: 978-0-664-22577-3 (alk. paper)
ISBN-10: 0-664-22577-2 (alk. paper)
1. Bible. N.T.—Introductions. I. Title.

BS2330.3 .G75 2003
225.6'1—dc21

2002035836

∞ The paper used in this publication meets the minimum requirements of the American National Standard for Information Sciences—Permanence of Paper for Printed Library Materials, ANSI Z39.48-1992.

This adult Bible study is dedicated to

Father Elias Chacour

Compatriot of Jesus, who walks daily where Jesus walked in Galilee,
man of God who builds on his dreams that God's children can live in peace,
champion of peace who teaches love and respect for all God's children,
founder of Mar Elias Educational Institutions in Ibillin, Galilee, Israel,
and dear friend, mentor, and colleague.

Contents

Introduction ix

Part 1
Participant's Guide 1

1 Introducing the New Testament 3
2 The Gospel of Matthew 16
3 The Gospel of Mark 26
4 The Gospel of Luke 34
5 The Gospel of John 45
6 The Acts of the Apostles 56
7 Epistles of the New Testament 68
8 The Revelation to John 77

Part 2
Leader's Guide 87

Guidelines for Bible Study Leaders 89
1 Introducing the New Testament 94
2 The Gospel of Matthew 102
3 The Gospel of Mark 110
4 The Gospel of Luke 116
5 The Gospel of John 122
6 The Acts of the Apostles 132
7 Epistles of the New Testament 140
8 The Revelation to John 147

Appendix 158

Introduction

You may have read the book *The Bible from Scratch: The Old Testament for Beginners*, or been in a Bible study class based on it. If so, you are familiar with the approach this book will take. If this book, and perhaps a study group you will be attending, is your first exposure to the topic, then you will discover a lot of new information about the New Testament and will experience an approach to its study that may be different from what you are accustomed to.

Do you have memories of your Sunday school teacher expecting you to memorize all of the books of the Bible in order? Can you still recite them?

Have you been in conversation with someone who quotes so many Bible verses that you feel intimidated and embarrassed about how little you know about the Bible?

Were you ever in a Bible study group when the leader instructed the class members to look up a Bible passage and you weren't quite sure how to do it?

Have you been invited by a friend or someone in your church to attend a Bible study group and you thought of many reasons not to go because you were sure you would feel out of place?

If you have answered one or more of the above questions in the affirmative, it may be that you have found the right resource to help you. After you have read this book, and perhaps been part of a group using the book for its study, you may not have memorized more Bible verses but you will find yourself becoming more comfortable with reading and studying the Bible. A research project[1] was conducted in the mid-1980s in which 3,567 adult members of 561 congregations were asked which topics they were "interested" or "very interested" to study. Of twenty-six possible topics, "The Bible" ranked the highest, with 77 percent indicating interest or high interest. If your church is anything like the ones I know, it is obvious that 77 percent of the adult members are not involved in Bible study classes, groups, or programs. It is more likely to be closer to 15 to 25 percent.

I think the adults represented by the 50 to 60 percent who expressed interest but are not involved in Bible study in our churches are sincere in their desire to study the Bible but for a variety of reasons they are not motivated to participate in such groups. Perhaps you can identify with those who would like to know more about the Bible but are reluctant to seek out a Bible study group or accept an invitation to attend one. I have heard such reluctance stated as: "I'm sure everyone else in the group will know more about the Bible than I do." "Whenever people talk about the Bible I get confused and have a lot of questions that I'm afraid to ask because they seem like stupid questions." "I can't keep up with those who know where to find Bible passages." "To learn my new computer program I bought *Microsoft Office for Dummies*. That's what I need for learning the Bible." This book is written to address the concerns represented by such statements.

My vision for teaching the Bible and my desire are that all believers become biblically literate so that they will be comfortable reading and studying the Bible and be able to enter into conversation with others about the Bible. By biblical literacy I mean several things:

- Having one's own Bible and reading it regularly
- Being able to find Bible passages and use the footnotes and cross-reference notes
- Being comfortable using Bible study tools such as an atlas, dictionary, and concordance
- Gaining a sense of the story line of the Bible
- Recognizing major characters and events in the Bible in the order of their appearance
- Seeing connections between the themes of the Old and New Testaments
- Relating the passages and stories of the Bible to one's own faith and life journeys
- Viewing events in the world and making decisions from a biblical perspective

This book, and the course you may be involved in, is one small effort to assist you in increasing your biblical literacy.

The Bible from Scratch: The New Testament for Beginners is written to address other needs as well. You may be among those who have been attending Bible study groups for a number of years where the study has focused on specific passages or stories or books of the Bible. You have enjoyed such studies but have wished for an overview of the Bible so that you could see the relationships between its various parts. Or you wish you could place the biblical events and characters in their historical context. If that is an interest of yours, this study guide will be a helpful resource.

Another value of this book may be to provide you with a refresher course where you review familiar material but look at it from a different perspective. Whatever brings you to this book, I pray that God will bless you by the portions of the Bible that you read, by the thinking you do guided by the questions, and by the prayers you are prompted to pray. If you would like to join with others in the adventure of exploring the Bible, consider taking the initiative to form a group of fellow pilgrims on the journey. Ask your pastor or a Bible study leader in your church to guide such a group. When you are able to do Bible study with others in a group in your church, you are almost guaranteed to receive even more blessings than if you do the study solo.

If you find this study to be of value you may be interested in exploring the companion study, *The Bible from Scratch: The Old Testament for Beginners*, also available from Westminster John Knox Press.

1. *Effective Christian Education: A National Study of Protestant Congregations*, funded by the Lilly Endowment and conducted by Search Institute, 1990.

Part One

PARTICIPANT'S GUIDE

Chapter One

Introducing the New Testament

Getting Started

This book is the second in a series. If you have already read or been in a study group with the first book, *The Bible from Scratch: The Old Testament for Beginners*, you may want to read this chapter quickly because much of the material is similar to chapter 1 of the first book. If you are coming to this book without benefit of the first one, then you will want to work through the chapter more carefully. This chapter deals with the New Testament as a whole. It sets the stage for reading and studying the remaining seven chapters, each of which focuses on a specific portion of the New Testament.

Prayer Prompted by Scripture

We follow the same pattern as we did in the first volume of this series. We begin each chapter with a prayer exercise that is prompted by one or more passages of the book or books of the New Testament that are the focus of the chapter. We begin each chapter in this way for at least three reasons:

1. To discern the most meaning from Scripture, we must approach the texts in a prayerful way.
2. The Bible is not just a book to read and study; it is also a book that "speaks" to us. We are able to hear its message when we are in a listening mode of prayer.
3. When we approach the Scriptures prayerfully, we will be more centered and ready for our reading and reflection.

The New Testament arose out of the life and ministry of the first generation of Christians in the early church. They were inspired by the life and teachings of Jesus and were empowered by the Holy Spirit to share the good news of the life, death, and resurrection of Jesus the Christ. The disciples and those who joined with them learned and taught, worshiped and worked, and healed and helped for many years before the first words were written that are now the collection of writings we know as the New Testament.

In Acts 2:42 we read, "They devoted themselves to the apostles' teaching and fellowship, to the breaking of bread and the prayers." In this passage we gain some clues regarding the life and ministry of the members of the emerging church. This verse is in the context of what happened on the Day of Pentecost, fifty days after Jesus' resurrection. The followers of Jesus were gathered in Jerusalem for the Pentecost celebrations when to their surprise they received the gift of the Holy Spirit. They were empowered to share the good news of that gift to all who were present. Before the day was over, three thousand people believed and were baptized. "They [the baptized ones] devoted themselves to the apostles' teaching and fellowship, to the breaking of bread and the prayers." In this one verse we gain some clues regarding life in the early church. Among the important aspects of their life together was prayer. In this book and course we continue in that tradition, with prayer being central to our life together in Christ.

Read Matthew 5:1–12, a passage we know as the Beatitudes. The word "beatitude" is from the Latin and means "blessing." In this passage there are nine blessings, each extended to a people with particular needs or circumstances. What follows is a litany based on the nine blessings. The first line of each blessing is quoted from the Contemporary English Version, and the second line is a prayer response reflecting the meaning of the second line in the biblical text.

God blesses those people who depend only on him.
I desire to be with you, dear God, you are my strength and my life.

God blesses those people who grieve.
I seek your comfort and love in my time of sorrow and despair.
God blesses those people who are humble.
Help me to continue to know my place of worth in your world.
God blesses those people who want to obey him more than to eat or drink.
You grant me more than I deserve and I am deeply grateful, gracious God.
God blesses those people who are merciful.
Remind me, O God, that I will be treated by others as I treat them.
God blesses those people whose hearts are pure.
I am unworthy and yet you receive me into your presence.
God blesses those people who make peace.
Remind me, God, that to be your child is to live in peace with all your children.
God blesses those people who are treated badly for doing right.
You welcome me into your realm, which is more important than anything else.
God will bless you when people insult you, mistreat you, and tell all kinds of evil lies about you because of me. (Write your own prayer response below.)

____

____

Take a few minutes to reflect on two questions:

What do these blessings say to us about God's love and grace?

What do these blessings teach us about our life commitments and responsibilities?

Approaching This Bible Study

If you come to this book and study without benefit of the first book in the series, then you may have some questions that I would like to answer briefly.

You may be thinking, "What can I expect in this course?" Some of the things you are likely to experience are:

- You will be on a quick journey through the whole New Testament. More time will be spent on some books than others. For a more in-depth study it will be necessary to find other resources. An excellent collection of resources for in-depth Bible study is published by The Kerygma Program.[1]

1. Send for a catalog to The Kerygma Program, 300 Mt. Lebanon Blvd., Suite 205, Pittsburgh, PA 15234. Check their Web site at www.kerygma.com.

- You may develop a lot of questions. Questions are good. Questions lead to understanding. Don't be bashful about having questions; ask them of your group leader if you are in a Bible study group, or search for your own answers using one or more of the resources suggested on pages 160–161.

- It is possible that this study will whet your appetite for more study. If so, you can count on an exciting venture as you head off in new directions prompted by this study.

- You may decide that you want to buy a new study Bible and/or some other tools to help you in your Bible study. See pages 159–160 for suggestions.

If you find these things happening to you, you will be well on your way to moving from beginner to Bible adventurer.

You may be wondering, "Which Bible should I use?" There are several ways to answer that question.

- You could use whichever Bible you have available (see pages 158–159 for a description of several Bible translations).
- If you have more than one Bible, you will find it helpful to use at least two different translations for your personal study. You will find that your understanding of Bible concepts and passages increases if you read from two or more translations.
- A study Bible will be a very helpful resource. You can find descriptions of several study Bibles on pages 159–160. Before purchasing a study Bible you may want to discuss several possibilities with your pastor, church educator, or class leader. Each study Bible has unique characteristics and features.

Another question you may have is, "What are some of the unique features of this Bible study book and course?" There are several ways to answer that question.

- As I write, I am not making any assumptions about how much you should already know about the Bible. Some of the material may be elementary for you, and if that is the case you will be able to move more quickly into new areas of Bible study. If some of the material is new to you, you will benefit from taking these simple steps into the Bible before you take the big steps or leaps. It is helpful to review and reinforce skills and information you already know.

- This book and course will combine basic Bible skills with basic information about the books of the New Testament. If you are part of a Bible study group, you will have opportunities to experience a wide variety of activities to increase your skills with and knowledge of the New Testament.
- Also, this book and course depend on you the reader, or group participant, investing yourself in the process. You will gain a lot if you take the time to do the activities in each chapter and participate actively in the various engaging activities that are a part of each session plan.

Looking at the Whole New Testament

Let's take the first step by opening your Bible to the table of contents. You will quickly find the listing of the twenty-seven books in the New Testament. Some of these books are only a few pages long, which means if you are not familiar with the order of the New Testament books you may have difficulty finding a book you are searching for. Never feel embarrassed to first turn to the table of contents when you want to find a book in the New Testament that may be new to you or is not easy to find. One word of caution: in some Bibles the numbering of the pages begins from page one again at the first page of the New Testament. This could be a little confusing if someone identifies a passage by a page number rather than the usual book, chapter, and verse process.

In most Bibles, after the table of contents, you will find a page with all of the books of the Bible in the order in which they appear, along with their corresponding abbreviations. Spend a few minutes skimming over the beginning pages of the Bible or just the New Testament. Make a list of some of the things you notice, and also write down any questions that come to mind. You can share some of the things on your lists during the group session, or you can discuss them with a friend at church. It may be that you will be led by your questions to search in other resources for answers. There is a list of helpful Bible study resources and tools on pages 160–161. Nothing you notice and no question is inappropriate.

Things I notice	Questions I have
________________	________________
________________	________________
________________	________________
________________	________________

Look again at the table of contents. You probably notice titles of books with strange names, some of which may even be difficult to pronounce. If you wonder how to pronounce any of the book names, be sure to ask for assistance in class. As you have noticed, the Bible is divided into two major sections: the Old Testament (also called the Hebrew Scriptures), with thirty-nine books, and the New Testament, with twenty-seven books. This book and course will focus on the New Testament. If you haven't read the Old Testament or studied it in a group, you may want to obtain *The Bible from Scratch: The Old Testament for Beginners* to work with after you have completed your study of the New Testament.

In addition to the two major sections (a total of sixty-six books) there is a variety of types of literature or types of writings represented by those books. Some books are more historical while others are more like poetry; some contain a lot of laws and others are words of prophecy; some are letters and others are Gospels. Through the following chapters of this book and the sessions in the course, we will explore examples of these various types of writings.

Look again at the list of New Testament books in the table of contents. The books were not necessarily written in the order that they appear. Rather, the list begins with four Gospels followed by the story in Acts of the early Christians after Jesus' resurrection. Then follows a list of letters or epistles, some of which are written to churches while others are addressed to individuals. Some are written by the apostle Paul and others by anonymous authors. The New Testament concludes with the book of Revelation.

Opening Your Bible to an Individual Book

Notice in the table of contents the page number for the beginning of the book of Matthew. Check to see whether your Bible has an introduction to the book of Matthew. Some Bibles, especially study Bibles, have introductory articles that provide background information on the dating, authorship, setting, theme, and outline of each book of the Bible. Turn to the first page of Matthew and look with a curious eye at the whole page and all the little things that are there. First, make a list of the major things you notice, and then write any questions that come to mind prompted by what you see on that page. If you are new to the Bible, don't hesitate to write down anything that comes to mind even if it seems obvious to you. If you are a veteran of Bible reading, look with more care and curiosity, and don't be afraid to write down anything that interests you.

Things I notice	Questions I have
________________	________________
________________	________________
________________	________________
________________	________________

Finding Books, Chapters, and Verses

Let's look at the matter of abbreviations and punctuation. Abbreviations sometimes differ from Bible to Bible. For instance, in the New Revised Standard Version (NRSV) you will see "Jon" for Jonah as compared to the New International Version (NIV), where you will see "Jnh." Sometimes there will be different abbreviations in several editions of the same translation. On page 13 you will find a list of the common abbreviations for the books of the Bible. It is helpful to become familiar with the particular abbreviations used in your Bible and to recognize that other Bibles may employ different letter symbols to identify the various books. Usually in Bible notes, footnotes, cross-references, and other citations of passages you will find abbreviations for names of the books rather than the complete spelling.

The matter of punctuation used in citing Bible verses and passages is also very important. Veteran Bible readers don't think twice about this matter, but if you are new to the Bible it will be helpful to review some of the most familiar ways to punctuate references to Bible passages. Notice the several examples in the chart on page 10.

Bible Skills and Tools Inventory

Take time before the next class to complete the Bible Skills and Tools Inventory found on page 12. All of the items refer to a skill or tool that is helpful for reading and studying the Bible. The results of this inventory when tabulated for the whole group will help your leader know what to emphasize and what to assume when planning future class sessions. There will be no judgment

Examples of Bible Passages' Punctuation

Matt. 2:1 We have the name of the book, followed by chapter 2, followed by a colon, which separates the chapter number from the verse number. Some Bibles use a period instead of a colon. Notice that the number for verse 1 does not usually appear in the text. The number for the first verse of every chapter is assumed, except in the book of Psalms.

Matt. 2:1–6 The dash means that we read chapter 2, verses 1 through 6.

Matt. 2:1–6, 13–15
The comma separates two distinct passages, which means that we read verses 1 through 6 and 13 through 15.

Matt. 2:1, 6, 9, 14, 20, and 26
This means that we read only the designated individual verses in chapter 2.

Matt. 5:43–48;
7:24–27; and 22:34–40
Passages separated by semicolons means that you read just the three passages that are listed.

Matt. 3:1–7a This designation is less common. You will notice that verse 7 has two parts, *a* and *b*. When you find a lowercase letter as part of a verse citation, it means you read only part of the verse. Some verses are longer and could have three or four parts, *a* to *d*.

of your proficiency or lack thereof with these skills and tools. During the sessions of the course you will be introduced to various Bible study skills and tools. If your group is large it may not be possible for each person to have separate volumes of Bible dictionaries, concordances, or other resources. If that is the case, have photocopied pages from such books so that you will be able to use them in your exploring. The leader of your group will bring to class examples of each of these Bible study tools. The most helpful tool of all for individuals to use in exploring the Bible is a study Bible.

Using a Bible Concordance

During the class session you will learn how to use a Bible concordance. A concordance is a book that contains all, or many, of the words of the Bible in alphabetical order with all or some of the verses that contain that word. The verses are presented in the order of the books of the Bible. There are three main types of concordances: 1. a very brief concordance that appears in the back of a study Bible, 2. a concise concordance that contains most of the key words of the Bible with representative key verses for those words, and 3. a comprehensive concordance that contains all of the words of the Bible with all of the verses in which each word appears. Professors, teachers, and pastors use a comprehensive concordance for intensive biblical study. A concise concordance will serve well for most others who engage in Bible study. You will see on pages 14–15 examples of listings from each of the three types of concordances featuring the word "law." Notice the number of verses in each example. The example of a comprehensive concordance includes only a portion of the verse references because to include them all would take more space than we have. However, you will see clearly the differences between the three types of concordances. In these days of personal computers many Bible students do not use a concordance in a book format. They have a version of the Bible installed on the hard drive of their computers and are able to find in seconds what might take minutes or hours to find using a concordance in book format.

Bible Skills and Tools Inventory

Each of the items below refers to a skill and/or tool that is helpful for studying the Bible. Check the statements in the column to the right that represent your own experience with the Bible.

1. Finding Bible passages by book, chapter, and verse is
   ___ no problem
   ___ sometimes difficult
   ___ a skill with which I need help

2. Identifying books of the Bible by their abbreviations is
   ___ no problem
   ___ sometimes difficult
   ___ a skill with which I need help

3. Checking the footnotes at the bottom of the pages of the Bible is a skill I use
   ___ often
   ___ occasionally
   ___ never

4. Using cross-reference notes to find sources or repetitions of passages in other places in the Bible is something I do
   ___ often
   ___ occasionally
   ___ never

5. Using a Bible dictionary is something I do
   ___ often
   ___ occasionally
   ___ never

7. Using a Bible commentary is something I do
   ___ often
   ___ occasionally
   ___ never

8. Using a Bible atlas is something I do
   ___ often
   ___ occasionally
   ___ never

9. Using different translations of the Bible is something I do
   ___ often
   ___ occasionally
   ___ never

10. The translations of the Bible I have are ______________________________.

11. The translation I prefer is ______________________________________.

12. Some things I hope this class will help me to learn or do with the Bible are
   ____
   ____.

Examples of Bible Books' Abbreviations

There should be a list of abbreviations that are used for the books of the Bible in the front of your Bible somewhere after the table of contents. Below are some commonly used abbreviations. A look at the list in your Bible will tell you which abbreviations your Bible uses.

Old Testament Books

Genesis	Ge	Gen
Exodus	Ex	Exod
Leviticus	Lv	Lev
Numbers	Nu	Num
Deuteronomy	Dt	Deut
Joshua	Js	Josh
Judges	Jg	Judg
Ruth	Ru	
1 Samuel	1 Sa	1 Sam
2 Samuel	2 Sa	2 Sam
1 Kings	1 Ki	1 Kgs
2 Kings	2 Ki	2 Kgs
1 Chronicles	1 Ch	1 Chron
2 Chronicles	2 Ch	2 Chron
Ezra	Ez	Eza
Nehemiah	Ne	Neh
Esther	Es	
Job	Jb	
Psalms	Ps	Psa
Proverbs	Pr	Prov
Ecclesiastes	Ec	Eccles
Song of Songs	SS	Song
Isaiah	Is	Isa
Jeremiah	Jr	Jer
Lamentations	La	Lam
Ezekiel	Eze	Ezek
Daniel	Da	Dan
Hosea	Ho	Hos
Joel	Jl	
Amos	Am	
Obadiah	Ob	Obd
Jonah	Jnh	Jon
Micah	Mi	Mic
Nahum	Na	Nh
Habakkuk	Hb	Hab
Zephaniah	Zep	Zeph
Haggai	Hg	Hag
Zechariah	Zec	Zech
Malachi	Ml	Mal

New Testament Books

Matthew	Mt	Matt
Mark	Mk	
Luke	Lk	
John	Jn	
Acts	Ac	
Romans	Ro	Rom
1 Corinthians	1 Co	1 Cor
2 Corinthians	2 Co	2 Cor
Galatians	Ga	Gal
Ephesians	Ep	Eph
Philippians	Php	Phil
Colossians	Col	
1 Thessalonians	1 Th	1 Thess
2 Thessalonians	2 Th	2 Thess
1 Timothy	1 Ti	1 Tim
2 Timothy	2 Ti	2 Tim
Titus	Tit	
Philemon	Phm	Philem
Hebrews	Hb	Heb
James	Ja	Jas
1 Peter	1 Pe	1 Pet
2 Peter	2 Pe	2 Pet
1 John	1 Jn	
2 John	2 Jn	
3 John	3 Jn	
Jude	Jd	
Revelation	Re	Rev

Three Different Concordances

In the two columns below, you will see examples of the differences between three types of concordances, featuring the word *law*. Notice that that word is represented by a boldface **l.** Verse citations from a concordance in a study Bible are very few and selective of key passages. In a concise concordance there are more verse citations, but they are still very limited and selective. In a complete concordance every verse with the word *law* is cited. If we were to add related words such as *laws, lawful,* and *lawless,* there would be many more citations.

Example as in a Study Bible

Exod.	24:12	I will give you the tablets of stone, with the **l**
Deut.	1:5	Moses undertook to expound this **l** as follows
	4:44	This is the **l** that Moses set before the Israelites
Josh.	1:8	This book of the **l** shall not depart out of your mouth
Ps.	1:2	their delight is in the **l** of the Lord
	119:97	Oh, how I love your **l**!
Jer.	31:33	I will put my **l** within them
Matt.	22:36	"Teacher, which commandment in the **l** is the greatest?"
Luke	24:44	everything written about me in the **l** of Moses
John	1:17	the **l** indeed was given through Moses.
Rom.	6:14	you are not under **l** but under grace.
	13:10	love is the fulfilling of the **l**.
Gal.	2:19	For through the **l** I died to the **l**.
	3:19	Why then the **l**?
Jas.	1:25	But those who look into the perfect **l**
	2:8	You do well if you really fulfill the royal **l** according to the scripture

Example as in a Concise Concordance

Exod.	12:49	there shall be one **l** for the native
Num.	5:29	This is the **l** in cases of jealousy
Deut.	4:44	This is the **l** that Moses set before the Israelites
	27:8	You shall write on the stones all the words of this **l**
	31:26	Take this book of the **l**
Josh.	8:34	And afterward he read all the words of the **l**
2 Kgs.	22:8	I have found the book of the **l** in the house of the Lord
Ezra	7:26	All who will not obey the **l**
Neh.	13:3	When the people heard the **l**
Ps.	1:2	their delight is in the **l** of the Lord
	19:7	The **l** of the Lord is perfect
	37:31	The **l** of their God is in their hearts
	119:44	I will keep your **l** continually
	119:97	Oh, how I love your **l**! It is my meditation all day long
Prov.	28:4	Those who forsake the **l** praise the wicked
	28:7	Those who keep the **l** are wise children
Jer.	26:4	walk in my **l** that I have set before you
	31:33	I will put my **l** within them
Matt.	5:17	I have come to abolish the **l** or the prophets
	12:5	have you not read in the **l** that on the Sabbath
Luke	2:39	finished everything required by the **l** of the Lord.
	5:17	Pharisees and teachers of the **l** were sitting near by
	10:26	What is written in the **l**? What do you read there?
	16:16	The **l** and the prophets were in effect until John came
John	1:17	The **l** indeed was given through Moses; grace and truth came through Jesus Christ
	8:5	in the **l** Moses commanded us to stone such women
Acts	6:13	This man never stops saying things against this holy place and the **l**
	13:15	After the reading of the **l** and the prophets
Rom.	2:13	For it is not the hearers of the **l** who are righteous in God's sight, but the doers of the **l** who will be justified
	3:31	Do we then overthrow the **l** by this faith? By no means!
	7:14	For we know that the **l** is spiritual
	8:3	For God has done what the **l** . . . could not do.
	13:10	love is the fulfilling of the **l**.
1 Cor.	9:21	To those outside the **l** I became as one outside the **l**
	15:56	The sting of death is sin, and the power of sin is the **l**.
Gal.	3:12	But the **l** does not rest on faith; on the contrary
	5:14	For the whole **l** is summed up in a single commandment
1 Tim.	1:8	Now we know that the **l** is good
Jas.	2:8	You do well if you really fulfill the royal **l** according to the scripture

Example as in a Complete Concordance

Exod. 12:49 there shall be one **l** for the native
24:12 I will give you the tablets of stone, with the **l**
Lev. 11:46 This is the **l** pertaining to land animal and bird
12:7 This is the **l** for her who bears a child, male or female
24:22 You shall have one **l** for the alien and for the citizen
Num. 5:29 This is the **l** in cases of jealousy
5:30 and the priest shall apply this entire **l** to her
6:13 This is the **l** for the nazirites when the time
6:21 This is the **l** for the nazirites who take a vow
15:16 You and the alien . . . shall have the same **l** and the same ordinance
15:29 you shall have the same **l** for anyone who acts in error
19:2 This is a statute of the **l** that the LORD has commanded
19:14 This is the **l** when someone dies in a tent
31:21 This is the statute of the **l** that the LORD has commanded
Deut. 1:5 Moses undertook to expound this **l** as follows
4:8 what other great nation has statutes and ordinances as just as this entire **l** that I am setting before you today?
4:44 This is the **l** that Moses set before the Israelites
17:11 You must carry out fully the **l** that they interpret for
17:18 When he has taken the throne of his kingdom, he shall have a copy of this **l** written for him
17:19 diligently observing all the words of this **l**
27:3 You shall write on them all the words of this **l** when you have crossed over, to enter the land
27:8 write on the stones all the words of this **l** very clearly.
27:26 Cursed be anyone who does not uphold the words of this **l** by observing them.
28:61 even though not recorded in the book of this **l**.
29:21 the covenant written in this book of the **l**.
29:29 to observe all the words of this **l**.
30:10 decrees that are written in this book of the **l**.
31:9 Then Moses wrote down this **l**, and gave it to the priests
31:11 you shall read this **l** before all Israel in their hearing
31:12 observe diligently all the words of this **l**
31:24 When Moses had finished writing down in a book the words of this **l** to the very end
31:26 Take this book of the **l** and put it beside the ark of the covenant of the LORD your God
32:46 diligently observe all the words of this **l**
33:4 Moses charged us with the **l**.
33:10 They teach Jacob your ordinances, and Israel your **l**.
Josh. 1:7 being careful to act in accordance with all the **l**
1:8 This book of the **l** shall not depart out of your mouth
8:31 as it is written in the book of the **l** of Moses
8:32 Joshua wrote on the stones a copy of the **l** of Moses
8:34 And afterward he read all the words of the **l** . . . according to all that is written in the book of the **l**
23:6 observe and do all that is written in the book of the **l**
24:26 Joshua wrote these words in the book of the **l** of God
1 Kgs. 2:3 as it is written in the **l** of Moses
2 Kgs. 10:31 But Jehu was not careful to follow the **l** of the LORD.
14:6 what is written in the book of the **l** of Moses.
17:13 in accordance with all the **l** that I commanded your
17:26 because they do not know the **l** of the god of the land
17:27 teach them the **l** of the god of the land
17:34 they do not follow the statutes or . . . the **l**
17:37 The statutes and the ordinances and the **l**
21:8 according to all the **l** that my servant Moses
22:8 I have found the book of the **l** in the house of the LORD

Chapter Two
The Gospel of Matthew

The first four books of the New Testament are identified as Gospels. "Gospel" is an English translation of a Greek word that means "good news." This refers to the good news preached by Jesus about the coming of the reign of God in the life of the world and among God's people. Gospel came to mean the message about Jesus Christ proclaimed by his followers. Later, the four books that appear first in the New Testament were called Gospels, thus the Gospel of Matthew, of Mark, of Luke, and of John. The Gospels are not biographies of the life of Jesus. Rather, they are witnesses to God's good news as seen in the life, teachings, passion, and resurrection of Jesus Christ.

Each of the four Gospels has unique characteristics and is addressed to a particular audience from a particular perspective. Thus, many differences exist among the Gospels even though they all give witness to the same reality. In this chapter we review some characteristics of all four Gospels and then focus primarily on summarizing the distinctive contents of Matthew. In the next three chapters we focus on the Gospels of Mark, Luke, and John separately.

Matthew, Mark, and Luke are referred to as the Synoptic Gospels. The word "synoptic" is from the Greek, *syn* meaning "together" and *optic* meaning "seeing," which suggests that we are to "see the three Gospels together." The reason for seeing them together is that there are many, many parallel passages where material in one Gospel is repeated in the other one or two. There are few parallel passages between John and the other three Gospels.

Prayer Prompted by Scripture

Matthew and Luke both contain the essence of what has become known to us as the Lord's Prayer. Pray the following words of the Lord's Prayer. This is known as the ecumenical version of the prayer.

Our Father in heaven,
hallowed be your name,
your kingdom come,
your will be done on earth as in heaven.
Give us today our daily bread.
Forgive us our sins as we forgive those who sin against us.
Save us from the time of trial and deliver us from evil.
For the kingdom, the power, and the glory are yours now and forever. Amen.

Read Matthew 6:9–15 and Luke 11:2–4. Compare the words of these two passages to notice their similarities and differences. Compare the words of the Lord's Prayer with which you are familiar with these two passages and also with the prayer printed above. Take a few minutes to reflect on the following questions. Use the space provided to write key words or phrases to summarize what you are thinking.

What can you remember about when you first learned the Lord's Prayer?

When you pray the Lord's Prayer, what is the meaning of that prayer for you?

The disciples asked Jesus to teach them to pray. What do you think Jesus wanted them to learn from praying the words he taught them?

Some Similarities and Differences between the Four Gospels

Before we focus on Matthew it will be helpful to do a general overview of all four Gospels. It is possible to summarize the story line of the four Gospels in four general categories; Introduction/Birth, Ministry, Passion, and Resurrection.

Review the following chart, which shows the number of chapters devoted to each of the four topics in each of the Gospels.

Some Similarities and Differences between the Four Gospels

Gospel	Intro/Birth	Ministry	Passion	Resurrection
Matthew 28 chapters	2	18	7	1
Mark 16 chapters	3 verses	10	5	8 verses
Luke 24 chapters	3	15½	4½	1
John 21 chapters	½	10½	8	2

When you review the chart you will notice several things:

- One quarter to one half of each Gospel is devoted to the passion and resurrection of Jesus. This suggests that the events in this relatively short period of time were very important to those who were writing and reading these Gospels. In fact, it could be argued that one of the primary reasons for the writers to write their Gospels was to respond to the question, "What does it mean that Jesus the Christ suffered, was crucified, and rose from the dead to be present again with his followers?"
- Only Matthew and Luke have genuine birth narratives. Mark has a very cryptic three-verse introduction and then launches into the narrative of Jesus' ministry. John's Gospel has a longer introduction of eighteen verses that is identified as the prologue to the Gospel. We will compare the birth narratives of Matthew and Luke in chapter 3.

- The resurrection narrative in Mark's Gospel is quite short, eight verses. Look at Mark 16:8. You will notice that there are notes that suggest two alternative endings to Mark. These endings are from additions to the original manuscripts at a later time. (We will work on the tool/skill of using footnotes later in this chapter.)

Important Features of the Four Gospels

In 1964 I accepted a call to the First Presbyterian Church of Livermore, California, to become their associate pastor for Christian education. I arrived at the church at a time when they were involved in a building program for a new sanctuary. The Communion table was placed in the middle of the sanctuary, with worshipers sitting on all four sides, the choir in the front, and the congregation in two transepts and nave. At the places where the walls intersected in the center of the cross-shaped building (cruciform) there were to be four very large faceted glass windows (thicker than stained glass and imbedded in cement rather than copper). The building committee decided the windows would depict the four Gospels. They spent weeks studying the Gospels in order to arrive at their understanding of the unique features of each Gospel. They gave their notes to the artist who would design the windows.

The result is four beautiful, somewhat abstract windows. The dominant color in the Matthew window (directly behind the pulpit) is blue and shows Jesus as a teacher. Green is the main color of the Mark window, which depicts Jesus as one who speaks and acts with authority. The primary color in the Luke window is red, portraying Jesus the healer. The John window is primarily yellow and gold and presents Jesus as the light of the world. I remember being very impressed with the hard work of the committee and how much they learned about the Gospels and how helpful they were to the artist.

In this chapter and the next three we summarize some of the important features of each Gospel by responding to four questions:

- Who is the author of the Gospel?
- What is the approximate date of the writing of the Gospel?
- What is the general structure or outline of the Gospel?
- What are several key features and/or themes of the Gospel?

It is important to realize that on the matter of authorship and dating of the Gospels there is much debate among the biblical scholars. What I share here is a general consensus of what the biblical scholars have concluded. A familiar phrase is "tradition suggests," which means that over the centuries there has developed considerable tradition associated with each Gospel, as well as other books in the New Testament. The tradition associated with a Gospel may or may not be supported by the latest scholarly research. It is not necessary for us to adopt precise conclusions about matters that scholars have debated for decades, and will continue to debate. What is important is for us to realize that the Gospels, as well as other books of the New Testament, are a collection of dynamic literature that represents the essence of who Jesus was and is, how the early church was formed, and what constituted faithful discipleship. What we learn from these ancient writings is instructive for us today as we seek to believe and live as faithful followers of Jesus the Christ. This collection of special books has inspired generation after generation of faithful people, throughout the world, in all walks of life, to believe in Jesus Christ as Lord and Savior and to live as his devoted followers.

An Overview of the Gospel of Matthew

Matthew's Gospel appears first in the New Testament. It has held a place of honor throughout the centuries. It was the most quoted of the Gospels by the church fathers. Matthew is to this day a favorite of many Christians, who can identify key persons, events, and passages more easily in Matthew than in the other Gospels. M. Eugene Boring writes, "The Gospel of Matthew, like all the New Testament Gospels, was composed as a literary work to interpret a theological meaning of a concrete historical event to people in a particular historical situation."[1] Whether or not the work was written by an eyewitness is not so important. However, it is very important that the Gospel was written by someone who was a devoted believer in Jesus as the Messiah, the one promised by God.

Tradition suggests that the apostle Matthew was the author of the Gospel bearing his name. Most biblical scholars, however, believe the author to be someone who remains anonymous. In the time when many books were being circulated and were considered for inclusion in the canon of Christian Scripture, it was not unusual to attribute an anonymous body of literature to some authoritative witness, in this case Matthew. It is surmised that the author was a prominent member of the Christian community in Antioch, the city where the followers of Jesus were first called "Christians" (Acts 11:26). The author was most

1. M. Eugene Boring, *The New Interpreter's Bible*, "The Gospel of Matthew Introduction" (Nashville: Abingdon Press, 1995).

likely someone of Jewish heritage who was very familiar with Hebrew Scriptures and the customs of the synagogue. The Gospel was addressed primarily to other Jews who would be impressed by Jesus' genealogy being traced back to Abraham (see Matt. 1:1–17). Jesus is presented by Matthew as a son of Abraham and son of David (Matt. 1:1). Many suggest that the Gospel was written toward the end of the first century, certainly after 70 CE[2], which was the date of the destruction of Jerusalem and the Temple by the Roman emperor Titus.

The Gospel of Matthew presents a series of narratives, each followed by a discourse of Jesus. Take time to skim the whole Gospel to notice the structure of the chapters as they alternate between narrative and discourse.

- Matt. 1–4: Following the genealogy there are the *narratives* of the birth of Jesus, the escape to Egypt, the return to Nazareth, John the Baptist, the baptism and temptation of Jesus, the beginning of his ministry, and the calling of the disciples.
- Matt. 5–7: These three chapters present the first *discourse*, known as the Sermon on the Mount, a collection of sayings of Jesus that reinterpret the old law and offer new expressions of the law. A repeated phrase is "You have heard that it was said . . . But I say to you." This section ends with the words, "Now when Jesus had finished saying these things, the crowds were astounded at his teaching, for he taught them as one having authority, and not as their scribes" (7:28–29).
- Matt. 8–9: After the discourse in the previous three chapters we see two chapters of *narratives* of healing, stilling a storm, calling Matthew, and responding to questions about fasting. Jesus heals a leper, a paralyzed man, a woman with a fever, many who were demon possessed, a paralytic, a girl who was thought to be dead, a hemorrhaging woman, two blind men, and a deaf mute.
- Matt. 10: In this chapter, the twelve apostles are named and then there is a *discourse* by Jesus in which he gives his disciples instructions regarding their mission as his representatives. The discourse ends with the words, "Now when Jesus had finished instructing his twelve disciples . . ." (11:1).

2. CE stands for "Christian Era" and is used more frequently now than AD.

- Matt. 11–12: There are *narratives* in these two chapters featuring John the Baptist, gathering of grain on the Sabbath, healings of a man with a withered hand and a demoniac, encounters with the scribes and Pharisees, and a visit from his mother and brothers.
- Matt. 13: Chapter 13 contains a *discourse* of seven parables of Jesus: Sower, Weeds, Mustard Seed, Yeast, Hidden Treasure, Pearl of Great Value, and the Net. In this chapter we learn of the purpose of Jesus teaching with parables and we see the only examples of Jesus explaining parables (the sower and the weeds). Jesus explains to his disciples his purpose for teaching in parables: "The reason I speak to them in parables is that 'seeing they do not perceive, and hearing they do not listen, nor do they understand'. . . . But blessed are your eyes, for they see, and your ears, for they hear" (13:13, 16).
- Matt. 14–17: The *narratives* of these four chapters contain several miracles: feeding of five thousand, Jesus walking on water, many healings, and feeding of four thousand. There are also stories of the death of John the Baptist, encounters with the authorities, Peter declaring Jesus as Messiah, and the transfiguration.
- Matt. 18: In this chapter we have a fourth *discourse* of Jesus that gives further instructions to the disciples, along with the parables of the Lost Sheep and the Unforgiving Servant. The discourse ends with the words, "When Jesus had finished saying these things, he left Galilee . . ." (19:1).
- Matt. 19–22: This long section is a mixture of *narratives* and *discourses*. We see amid the narratives five parables: Laborers in the Vineyard, the Fig Tree, Two Sons, the Wicked Tenants, and the Wedding Banquet. The narratives are Jesus blessing the children, an encounter with a rich young man, healing of a blind man, Jesus' entry into Jerusalem, cleansing of the temple, and dealing with questions about paying taxes and the resurrection. A short but significant passage is Jesus being tested by a Pharisee with a question about which was the greatest of the commandments. Jesus' answer is the familiar passage, "You shall love the Lord your God with all your

heart . . . soul . . . mind. And a second is like it: 'You shall love your neighbor as yourself'" (22:34–40).

- Matt. 23–25: These are three long chapters with long *discourses* by Jesus where he denounces the scribes and Pharisees and speaks of the destruction of the temple and about the end times. We also read three long parables of the Ten Bridesmaids, the Talents, and Separating the Sheep from the Goats.
- Matt. 26–28: The last three chapters contain the *narratives* of the plot to kill Jesus, his anointing at Bethany, betrayal by Judas, the Passover with the disciples, Peter's denial, Jesus' praying in Gethsemane, trials before the high priest and Pilate, the crucifixion and burial, and the resurrection appearances. The conclusion of Matthew is known as the Great Commission where Jesus charges his followers to go and make disciples, to baptize and teach, and to remember that he would remain with them forever.

Practicing with Footnotes

Most Bibles include footnotes throughout the chapters of the sixty-six books. Skim through the pages of the Gospel of Matthew and you will notice many footnotes serving a variety of purposes. Look at several examples from the NRSV. (The NRSV Bible I used had the footnote letters as indicated. However, in other editions of the NRSV, you may find different letters for the same footnote.)

- Matt. 1:1: "An account of the genealogy [a] of Jesus the Messiah, [b] the son of David, the son of Abraham." Look at the bottom of the page and you will see footnote "*a* Or *birth*" and "*b* Or *Jesus Christ*." This means that the Greek word in the text can be translated in two different ways. The words in the text are what the translators determined are the preferred translation, with the words in the footnotes being an alternative translation.
- Matt. 11:5: "The blind receive their sight, the lame walk, the lepers[j] are cleansed . . ." This footnote provides the additional information, "*j* The terms *leper* and *leprosy* can refer to several diseases."

- Matt. 11:9: "What then did you go out to see? A prophet? [l]" The explanation of this footnote contains a phrase that is repeated often throughout the Bible: "Other ancient authorities read . . ." Since there are no original manuscripts of biblical texts, the only texts available were written many centuries after the originals. There are many such manuscripts and, as might be expected, there are minor variations among them. I think it is a "miracle" that there is as much consistency among the many different manuscripts as there is, and that the variations are relatively minor.
- Matt. 23:13–15: If you read carefully verses 13 through 15 you will notice there is no verse 14. Instead there is a footnote *o* with the notation, "Other authorities add here (or after verse 12) verse 14, *Woe to you, scribes and Pharisees, hypocrites! For you devour widows' houses and for the sake of appearance you make long prayers; therefore you will receive the greater condemnation.*" There are several places in the Gospels where such notes appear and the omitted text is contained in a footnote. The most familiar example is the narrative of the woman caught in adultery (John 7:52–8:11). Sometimes the narrative is in the footnote or, as in the NRSV, is included in the body of the text, but with brackets and the footnote states, "The most ancient authorities lack 7:53–8:11."
- At Mark 16:8–9, you will see two alternative endings to the Gospel; a shorter ending and a longer one. Both endings are in brackets and the footnotes suggest other possible texts are included even in the longer alternative ending.

Comparing the Matthew and Luke Birth Narratives

The Gospels of Matthew and Luke are the only ones to include narratives of the birth of Jesus (Matt. 1:18–2:12 and Luke 2:1–20). When we hear or tell the story of Jesus' birth we tend to think of it as one story whereas in point of fact there are two very different stories with many different characters and events. On page 108 you will find a form to use to compare the two narratives. You will notice the differences when you apply the same questions to each of the narratives. The questions are:

1. Where did Mary and Joseph live?
2. In what city was Jesus born?
3. Where in the city was Jesus born?
4. Why did Mary and Joseph go to Bethlehem?
5. What ruler is mentioned?
6. Is a star mentioned?
7. Are angels mentioned?
8. Who comes to Bethlehem to visit Jesus?
9. What do they bring?
10. What voices of authority are quoted?

After you have answered all of the questions, what differences and similarities do you notice? What do you think is the significance of the differences? What are some ways to account for them?

Chapter Three
The Gospel of Mark

Even though Mark appears second in the order of the four Gospels, it was the first to be written. Matthew and Luke were written later and their authors had access to Mark. When we compare these three Gospels, we discover that almost 90 percent of Mark is repeated in Matthew and about 50 percent appears in Luke. Other material exists that is the same in Matthew and Luke but does not appear in Mark. Bible scholars have hypothesized that Matthew and Luke had before them another unnamed source that has been identified as *Q*, derived from the German word *Quelle*, meaning "source." In the prologue to Luke (1:1–4) the writer implies that he has taken into account what others have written previously.

In this chapter we review the structure and outline of Mark. You will notice that Mark has two distinctive sections of almost equal length. In addition to gaining an overview of the outline and content of the Gospel, we compare one passage in Mark with parallel passages in Matthew and in Luke in order to identify the similarities and differences between them.

Prayer Prompted by Scripture

One of the characteristics of Mark is that there are very few long discourses by Jesus. On the other hand, many encounters take place between Jesus and other people, and his words to them are very direct and clear. For our Prayer Prompted by Scripture activity, we are going to read a brief passage. Then, we quote a selected saying of Jesus to a person in the passage. You will see space after each quote for you to write a brief personal prayer response to those words of Jesus. Put yourself in the place of the one to whom Jesus is speaking and imagine that he is speaking those words to you. How will you respond to Jesus? What words will express your prayer? The first passage, the words of Jesus, and the prayer response are presented as an example of what you can do.

Read Mark 2:1–12 about Jesus forgiving and healing a paralytic: Jesus said to the paralytic, "Son, your sins are forgiven."

Prayer response:

O God, I wonder what I have done to deserve the gift of your forgiveness, and then I realize there is nothing I can do to justify or earn your forgiveness. You forgive me because you love me and desire for me to love you with my whole being. Thank you, gracious God, for blessing me with such undeserved love.

Read Mark 4:35–41 about Jesus stilling the storm: Jesus said to the disciples, "Why are you afraid? Have you still no faith?"

Prayer response:

Read Mark 8:27–30 about Peter's confession of Jesus as the Messiah: Jesus said, "But who do you say that I am?"

Prayer response:

Read Mark 10:13–16 about Jesus and the children: Jesus said, "Whoever does not receive the kingdom of God as a little child will never enter it."

Prayer response:

Read Mark 10:32–45 about the discussion of who is to be closest to Jesus in the kingdom: Jesus said, "Whoever wishes to become great among you must be your servant."

Prayer response:

An Overview of the Gospel of Mark

Turn to chapter 1 of Mark's Gospel and then skim through to the last chapter. You will notice several things as you skim:

- Mark's Gospel is the shortest of the four.
- There is no birth narrative as in Matthew and Luke. Mark begins with a quote from the prophet Isaiah and then a brief narrative about John the Baptist and Jesus' baptism by John. By Mark 1:14 Jesus is in Galilee and has begun his ministry of "proclaiming the good news."
- When you look at Mark 16:1–8 you notice that the resurrection narrative is very short. The tomb is empty and a "young man" announces that Jesus "has been raised," that he has gone ahead to Galilee. The tomb is empty but no resurrection appearances of the risen Christ follow.
- The original version of Mark ended at 16:8. Many years later, however, as the Gospel was being circulated, those believing that the original was insufficient added two other endings.

Even though the Gospel carries the name Mark, there is no conclusive internal evidence as to who the author "Mark" might be. Tradition suggests that the writer Mark was a companion of Peter in Rome and that he learned about Jesus' life, ministry, death, and resurrection from Peter (1 Pet. 5:13). In Acts a man identified as John Mark accompanied Paul and Barnabas on the first missionary journey but for some reason left them. A disagreement between Paul and Barnabas developed because John Mark had abandoned the journey and Paul refused to have Mark accompany them on a second journey. The disagreement was so intense that Paul and Barnabas split and went their separate ways. Paul took Silas, and Mark accompanied Barnabas. Mark is identified as Barnabas's cousin (Col. 4:10). It is not clear whether the John Mark of Acts and the Mark mentioned in 1 Peter are the same person. The consensus of biblical scholars is that Mark was the first of the Gospels to be written and was written sometime before 70 CE, the time of the destruction of Jerusalem and the temple by the Romans. Mark was a source used by both Matthew and Luke, thus accounting for the parallel passages between the three Gospels.

A key passage is Mark 8:27–30. In a sense this is the "hinge" passage of the Gospel. Read the passage carefully. If you have a study Bible or a commentary to accompany your reading, check out all the notes related to this passage. Jesus is with his disciples. He inquires of them regarding what people are saying about him. They report that some think he is John the Baptist, others think he is Elijah, and others think he is one of the other prophets who have returned from the dead. Jesus is not satisfied with their answers, so he asks them directly, "But who do you say that I am?" Peter answers for himself and the group, "You are the Messiah." The word "messiah" in Hebrew means "anointed one" and is translated into the Greek as *christos*, from which we derive the word "Christ." It is more accurate to say "Jesus the Christ" than to say "Jesus Christ." It is not as if *Christ* is his last name, but rather it is a description of who he is, the Messiah, the one anointed to deliver the faithful people of God from oppression. This passage, culminating in Peter's declaration of Jesus as the Christ, divides the Gospel into two parts. What follows is a summary of the content and emphases of each of the two parts.

Part 1 is Mark 1:1–8:26. In this part, after the introduction in 1:1–13, all of the action occurs in Galilee. Jesus healed many people, called and commissioned his disciples, taught in the synagogue and with parables, and experienced many conflicts. In addition to the healings there are several miracles in this section: stilling the storm (4:35–41), feeding the five thousand (6:30–44), walking on water (6:45–56), and feeding four thousand (8:1–10).

Already in chapter 1 the report is that the people "were astounded at his teaching, for he taught them as one having authority, and not as the scribes" (1:22). "His fame began to spread throughout the surrounding region of Galilee" (1:28). In chapter 2, questions are raised by the Pharisees regarding Jesus not following the laws of fasting and the Sabbath so that by 3:6, "The Pharisees went out and immediately conspired with the Herodians against him [Jesus], how to destroy him." The popularity of Jesus grew among the people of Galilee to the point where Jesus tried to get away from the crowds on several occasions. But the people always found him. On the other hand, there was a growing plot to condemn Jesus because he didn't observe the laws of Moses as strictly as the religious authorities expected him to do. The stage was being set for the second half of the Gospel, which is devoted exclusively to his last days.

You will find the following exercise revealing about the impact of Jesus on those he encountered along the way. Take a blank sheet of paper and draw five columns, each column with a heading like what follows. If you have time, read the first eight chapters of Mark carefully. If you are limited in the time you can spend on this exercise, skim the eight chapters in order to fill in the blanks for each column. (There may not always be something in the text to help you answer the question in the fifth column.) Even if you don't have time to create this chart for all eight chapters, take the time to work on one or two chapters. Follow the example as printed below.

Chapter and verse	Person(s) Jesus encountered	The setting of the encounter	The results of the encounter	What was said of Jesus?
1:16–20	Simon, Andrew, James, and John, four fishermen	Along the shore of the Sea of Galilee	Immediately he called them to follow him, and they did.	
1:21–28	People in the synagogue; a man with an unclean spirit	The synagogue in Capernaum on the Sabbath day	The man with the unclean spirit is healed.	They were all amazed. "What is this? A new teaching!"
2:15–17	Levi the tax collector, and scribes of the Pharisees	Dinner in Levi's house	Criticism of Jesus	"Why does he eat with tax collectors and sinners?"

Whether you have filled in information for three or four more narratives or you have filled up several pages, review the results of your work by reflecting on several questions:

How would you characterize the intent of Jesus' actions and statements?

What do you observe about the ways people responded to Jesus?

What comparisons do you make to the way people respond to Jesus today?

Part 2 is Mark 8:31–16:8. Prior to Peter's declaration of Jesus as Messiah, his entire ministry is conducted in the region of Galilee. From that time forward Jesus' ministry leads him to Jerusalem and his last days with his followers. Part 1 represents two-plus years of Jesus' ministry, and part 2 is a relatively short period of time. Jesus began to teach Peter and the others, after they acknowledged him as the Messiah, that he will "undergo great suffering, and be rejected by the elders, the chief priests, and the scribes, and be killed, and after three days rise again" (8:31). The disciples state that they will not let any harm come to Jesus, but he knows otherwise.

Chapters 9 to 12 include the transfiguration, one parable (the Vineyard), two healings (a boy possessed of spirits and blind Bartimaeus), a variety of encounters (children, a rich man, James and John, a widow, and religious authorities), two more predictions of his suffering and death, and challenges to Jesus' authority (regarding the baptism of John, the resurrection, the greatest commandment, and paying of taxes). Chapter 13 is a discourse in which Jesus speaks about the times to come and the last days. Chapters 14 and 15 contain all the narratives of the final plot to kill Jesus, the Passover meal with his disciples, the betrayal by Judas, trials before the high priest and Pilate, and his crucifixion. Mark concludes with a brief account of the empty tomb in 16:1–8.

Several other features of the Gospel of Mark are worth noting:

- Jesus is seen from beginning to end as a man with unique authority. His authority is from God and is expressed through words and deeds. It is an authority that is a unique expression of wisdom and truth, that interprets and enacts the spirit of the law rather than the letter of the law, and that is not intimidated by the threats of religious and political leaders. Jesus' authority is demonstrated by his ability to heal, to exorcise demons, to control elements of nature, to interpret the law according its original intent, and to challenge the presuppositions of the religious and political leaders of his day.
- Mark employs the word "immediately" seventeen times, which suggests Jesus is a man of decisive action and evokes quick responses from others. One gets a sense of urgency regarding the words and actions of Jesus. I once preached a sermon titled, "How Fast Is Immediate?" One of the conclusions I came to was that Mark was not so concerned to present all of the details of an encounter or an event, but rather summarized the important parts of a story and moved quickly to the conclusion with the word "immediately." I am sure much more was involved in every event or encounter than what is presented by Mark. He is not as interested in the details as he is in the results. Thus, "immediately" serves as a device to conclude a narrative or to make a transition to another.
- The Gospel of Mark presents Jesus as one who is often the center of conflicts. Sometimes the conflicts are with the religious leaders over his interpretation of the law. Jesus focused primarily on the *spirit* of the law whereas the scribes and Pharisees tended to emphasize obeying the *letter* of the law. The religious leaders also objected to Jesus associating with sinners and tax collectors, but Jesus' response was, "I have come to call not the righteous but sinners" (2:17). Jesus experienced conflicts

with his disciples because they did not fully understand his mission. They wanted to protect him from harm, but Jesus needed no protection from them. Jesus was clear about his mission and was not to be deterred from going to Jerusalem though his followers did not understand his ultimate intentions.

- Another feature of the Gospel of Mark is the emphasis on what is expected of those who would be obedient followers of Jesus the Christ. Characteristics of true discipleship include:

> "If any want to become my followers, let them deny themselves and take up their cross and follow me" (8:34).
>
> "Whoever wants to be first must be last of all and servant of all" (9:35).
>
> "Truly I tell you, whoever does not receive the kingdom of God as a little child will never enter it" (10:15).
>
> "You shall love the Lord your God with all your heart, and with all your soul, and with all your mind, and with all your strength. . . . You shall love your neighbor as yourself" (12:30–31).

The Great Commandment: Comparing Three Gospels

A very familiar passage identified as the Great Commandment concludes persons are to love God with heart, mind, soul, and strength, and their neighbors as themselves. The assumption is that Jesus is asked to identify the greatest commandment in an effort to trap him into naming one of the commandments and thus being guilty of misusing the law. However, when one compares this passage where it appears in Matthew, Mark, and Luke, we discover that our assumption is supported by only one Gospel and in the other two something very different is presented. With many familiar passages that appear in more than one Gospel, our memory often combines two or more parallel passages or selects one to be our understanding of the passage(s). When we compare parallel passages, we often get a very different picture and our understanding is enhanced by the similarities and differences that we observe.

The passage of the Great Commandment appears in Matthew 22:34–46, Mark 12:28–34, and Luke 10:25–42. In order to compare the passages we need to ask the same questions of each:

- What is the setting?
- Who is present?
- Who asks the question about the commandments?
- Why does the person ask the question?
- Who answers the question?
- What happens next?

When you answer all of the questions for each of the Gospels, you discover some very interesting things. There are three discoveries to mention at this point. First, in Matthew and Luke a lawyer asks Jesus a question to try to trap or test him. In Mark, a scribe asks Jesus the question because he observes that Jesus has given good answers to other questions. Second, in Luke the lawyer does not ask a question about which is the greatest commandment but rather asks about eternal life. It is Jesus who asks the lawyer the question, "What is written in the law?" to which the lawyer responds by quoting the commandments about loving God and neighbor. And third, in Luke the lawyer asks another question: "And who is my neighbor?" to which Jesus responds by telling the parable of the Good Samaritan.

If you are engaged in a group Bible study, you may be doing an exercise to compare the three Synoptic Gospels regarding this narrative dealing with the Great Commandment. Or, if you are not in a group you could do the exercise yourself by completing the chart on page 115.

Chapter Four
The Gospel of Luke

In this chapter we review an outline of the Gospel of Luke and identify several themes that are prominent in Luke. We need to remind ourselves that we are not doing an in-depth study but are trying to get a sense of the "lay of the land" of the New Testament and its major books. We also spend a little time working on the skill of using cross-reference notes.

Prayer Prompted by Scripture

When we study the Gospels and reflect on the life and ministry of Jesus, we discover that from his birth to death and resurrection Jesus was on a journey. The motif of journey is one with which we can also identify when we realize that we are on a spiritual journey our whole life long. Some of us are very aware that we are on a journey, and we are very intentional about how we travel that journey. Others of us are not as intentional, and we are often unaware of the nature of the journey we are on. For our prayer we are going to read several passages that mark critical moments in Jesus' spiritual journey and then meditate on those words as we reflect on their implications for our spiritual journeys. Take the time necessary to read the following passages and then to write a sentence or two as your response to each question. The suggested passages are very brief, so you may find it helpful to read a little more of the text that precedes and/or follows the verses that are listed.

Birth: Read Luke 2:8–14
How does the birth of a baby give you a sense of hope and promise?

Growth: Read Luke 2:52
What are some of the contributing factors to your growing in wisdom?

Baptism: Read Luke 3:21–22
What does your baptism mean to you?

Temptation: Read Luke 4:1–4
Are there any passages of Scripture that help you face your temptations?

Mission: Read Luke 4:14–21
What passages of Scripture provide you with a sense of your call to ministry?

Identity: Read Luke 9:18–20
What words would you use to declare your understanding of and faith in Jesus?

Commitment: Read Luke 13:31–33
How committed are you to trust God in the face of threats and troubles?

Communion: Read Luke 22:14–20
What memories do you associate with being present at the Lord's Table?

Death: Read Luke 23:44–47
In what ways does Jesus' death affect your life and faith?

New Life: Read Luke 24:28–32
What is your sense of the risen Christ being in your midst?

An Outline of the Gospel of Luke

There are seven major sections to the narrative of Jesus' birth, ministry, death, and resurrection as told by the author of the Gospel of Luke. The sections are not of equal length, but they are distinctive as to the literary structure of the Gospel. I am following the outline as presented in volume 9 (*Luke and John*) of the *New Interpreter's Bible*.

1. The prologue (Luke 1:1–4)

This is the shortest section of the Gospel; it consists of just one sentence. The author is not identified. However, tradition has suggested that Luke, the beloved physician and a companion of Paul (Col. 4:14), is the author. The author states explicitly that there are several accounts of the events surrounding the ministry of Jesus and that he desires to write an orderly account for a person named Theophilus, which in Greek means "friend of God." Theophilus may have been a person of high social standing who supported Luke in his writing of the Gospel, as well as of a second volume, the Acts of the Apostles. Or perhaps Theophilus is not a specific person but every person who is a "friend of God." The purpose for writing the Gospel is for the reader to "know the truth concerning the things about which you have been instructed" (1:4).

2. The birth narratives (Luke 1:5–2:52)

In these two chapters we have the annunciation, birth, naming, and circumcision of two infant boys, John and Jesus. Both mothers, Elizabeth and Mary, are visited by the angel Gabriel and surprised with an announcement that by God's gracious act they would give birth to special sons, Elizabeth in her old age and Mary in her youth.

Both Luke and Matthew tell of the birth of Jesus. However, the two narratives are quite different, as is the material surrounding the narratives. When we read, hear, and celebrate the birth of Jesus at Christmas, we tend to treat the birth as if it were one narrative when in fact there are two, as we discovered in the exercise we did in chapter 2.

3. Preparation for ministry (Luke 3:1–4:13)

In this section you find a description of John the Baptist's ministry, Jesus' baptism, the lineage of Jesus, and Jesus' temptation in the wilderness. You should notice two important things in this section. First of all, Jesus' lineage is traced through his father, with Joseph's line going from Jesus all the way back to Adam. This is in contrast to the lineage in Matthew, where it is traced from Abraham to Jesus.

Second, notice the way Jesus responds to the tempter in the desert wilderness during his forty days of fasting. He is tempted three times and each time he resists the temptation by saying, "It is written . . ." and proceeds to quote from the Scriptures, specifically the book of Deuteronomy. If your Bible has cross-reference notes, you will see that Jesus quotes from Deuteronomy 8:3: "One does not live by bread alone"; from Deuteronomy 6:13: "Worship the Lord your God, and serve only him"; and from Deuteronomy 6:16: "Do not put the Lord your God to the test." An interesting observation is that the words from Deuteronomy are words of Moses spoken after the forty-year journey in the wilderness and just before the Israelites were to cross over the Jordan into Canaan. The words are spoken after a time of trial and testing before beginning a whole new era of life and service in a new land. I believe that the author of Luke was very intentional in making the connection between Jesus' struggle in the wilderness and the Israelites' struggle. Jesus also is about to begin a new era of life and ministry across the Jordan in the land of Galilee and Judah.

4. Ministry in Galilee (Luke 4:14–9:20)

Immediately after Jesus' faithful conclusion to his time of testing in the wilderness the text reads, "Then Jesus, filled with the power of the Spirit, returned to Galilee, and a report about him spread through all the surrounding country" (Luke 4:14). He went to Nazareth where he lived as a child and young man. He launched his ministry by reading the Scriptures in the synagogue on a Sabbath day. He read from the prophet Isaiah: "The Spirit of the Lord is upon me, because he has anointed me to bring good news to the poor. He has sent me to proclaim release to the captives and recovery of sight to the blind, to let the oppressed go free, to proclaim the year of the Lord's favor" (Luke 4:18–19). There was nothing unusual about this event except that when he laid down the scroll Jesus went on to say, "Today this scripture has been fulfilled in your hearing" (Luke 4:21b.) By declaring himself the fulfillment of these words of Isaiah, Jesus so angered the people that they drove him out of town and threatened to kill him because they thought his words were blasphemous. However, he walked through the crowd without harm.

For the next five chapters Luke shows Jesus conducting his ministry in the Galilee region of Israel. He performs many miracles of healing and shows his mastery over nature by stilling a storm, over demons by driving them out of the Gerasene demoniac, and over death by raising the child of Jairus. He calls his disciples to join him in his ministry. He taught with parables and also by his actions. Jesus was confronted by the religious leaders and challenged regarding his observance of the laws of fasting and the Sabbath and also for associating with outcasts and sinners. He began to prepare his followers for what awaited him beyond Galilee in Jerusalem, that he would suffer for his obedience to God's call to faithfulness.

Toward the end of this section are two encounters that reveal the true nature of Jesus' identity and ministry. The first encounter (Luke 9:18–22) was when the disciples were asked by Jesus, "Who do the crowds say that I am?" After hearing several reports he asked more directly, "But who do you say that I am?" Peter answered, "The Messiah of God." The Hebrew word for "messiah" means "one who is anointed" for special service. The same word in Greek is *christos*, from which we derive the word "Christ." As we mentioned earlier, it is more accurate to speak of "Jesus the Christ" than it is to say "Jesus Christ" as if they were his first and last name. After Peter's declaration of Jesus as the Messiah, Jesus reveals to the disciples that he going to "undergo great suffering, and be rejected by the elders, chief priests, and scribes, and be killed, and on the third day be raised."

The second encounter is known as the transfiguration, where Jesus and three of his closest disciples (Peter, James, and John) are together on a mountain praying. The disciples experience Jesus in a radiant presence along with Moses and Elijah. In this dreamlike state, and overcome by a numinous presence, the disciples hear a voice say to them, "This is my Son, my Chosen; listen to him!"

Jesus' ministry in Galilee concludes by the healing of a child with an unclean spirit, by Jesus saying he is going to be betrayed, and by responding to an argument about who is the greatest.

5. Journey to Jerusalem (Luke 9:51–19:27)

This section begins with the words, "When the days drew near for him to be taken up, he set his face to go to Jerusalem" (Luke 9:51). The route and the duration of the journey are not clear, but it is clear that he is heading toward Jerusalem from this time forward. In Luke 13:22 we read, "Jesus went through one town and village after another, teaching as he made his way to Jerusalem." Luke 14:25 reports that "large crowds were traveling with him." Again, we read, "On the way to Jerusalem Jesus was going through the region between Samaria and Galilee" (Luke 17:11).

The journey toward Jerusalem concludes with two passages. First, there is the encounter with Zacchaeus in Jericho where this tax collector, despised by the people, repents and is blessed by Jesus with the promise of salvation. Second is a parable about ten servants who were entrusted to be good stewards of the master's money while he was away. The preface to the parable states that Jesus "was near Jerusalem." This is the longest of the seven sections of the Gospel of Luke. It is likely, however, that Jesus spent more time in Galilee than he did on his journey to Jerusalem.

This large section is filled with many accounts of Jesus teaching much of which appears in other settings in Matthew and Mark. He teaches the crowds, the disciples, and the religious leaders. Much of the teaching is done with parables. Of the twenty-six parables in Luke, nineteen of them are in this section. The most familiar parables are the Good Samaritan (10:29–37), the Great Banquet (14:15–24), and the Lost Sheep, Lost Coin, and Lost Son (15:1–32).

Chapter 11 begins with Luke's version of the Lord's Prayer, followed by his casting out demons from a mute person. The last half of the chapter includes six woes directed at the Pharisees and the lawyers. Jesus was not a very polite guest when the Pharisees invited him to have a meal with them. They criticize Jesus for not observing the ritual of washing before dinner and then he in turn accuses them, and the lawyers, of misusing their authority, worrying about trivialities of the law and forgetting about the intent of the law, and not living the righteous lives expected of them. From this point in the narrative to the end there are many references to Jesus being watched carefully so that those who object to his teachings and actions might be able to find fault with him and bring charges against him.

6. Ministry in Jerusalem: Teaching in the temple (Luke 19:28–21:38)

This section begins with Jesus' entry into Jerusalem coming down from the Mount of Olives (which we commemorate in Palm Sunday services) and ends with the report of Jesus teaching every day in the temple and spending the nights on the Mount of Olives. In addition to Jesus' entry into Jerusalem and subsequent cleansing of the temple, this short section includes the parable of the Wicked Tenants, predictions of future events, and a number of questions asked of him. The period of time between the procession into the city and the eve of Passover is just a few days.

Luke 20:20 shows the mood of the city and the desire of the authorities to develop a case against Jesus in order to arrest him: "So they watched him and sent spies who pretended to be honest, in order to trap him by what he said, so as to hand him over to the jurisdiction and authority of the governor." He is questioned regarding whether it is lawful to pay taxes to the emperor. The Sadducees do not believe in the resurrection, so they try to trap Jesus by asking a question about whose wife a woman will be in the resurrection if seven husbands died before the woman. In each instance Jesus turns the question back on the inquirer and states a truth with which they cannot argue.

Chapter 21 begins with a four-verse narrative of Jesus observing a poor widow putting two small coins in the temple treasury. He used this event as a device for teaching that the poor woman's offering was greater than all of the offerings of the rich people because she gave out of her poverty. This section ends with the words, "Every day he was teaching in the temple, and at night he would go out and spend the night on the Mount of Olives, as it was called. And all the people would get up early in the morning to listen to him in the temple" (Luke 21:37–38).

7. The passion and resurrection narratives (Luke 22:1–24:53)

The three chapters of this last section are packed with drama, intrigue, mystery, and hope. The narratives of this section include the Last Supper, Jesus' announcement of his betrayal and Peter's denial, praying in the Garden of Gethsemane, Jesus' arrest, Peter's denial of Jesus, Jesus on trial, the crucifixion and burial, the resurrection, the appearance on the road to Emmaus, Jesus' final appearance to the disciples, and his departure.

There are several "windows" through which to view the events of these last days of Jesus. One of the "windows" is to focus on the disciples. They are involved in almost every scene.

- The disciples were gathered with Jesus at the table to celebrate the Passover feast. After the traditional meal Jesus took the bread and the cup to call the disciples' attention to them as representing his body and his blood.
- A dispute arose among the disciples as they tried to determine which of them would be regarded as the greatest. Jesus admonished them that the ones who serve will be the greatest.
- Despite Peter swearing his allegiance to Jesus, he was told by Jesus that before the cock crows in the morning Peter will have denied him three times.
- Jesus and the disciples went to the Mount of Olives to pray. Jesus agonized about what was to occur and then discovered the disciples had fallen asleep.
- Judas came forward to identify Jesus and delivered him into the custody of the arresting party.
- As the soldiers came to the garden to arrest Jesus, one of his disciples tried to protect Jesus with a sword and cut off the ear of the servant of the high priest.
- Peter followed at a distance and was near where they had taken Jesus. He was questioned about his association with Jesus but vehemently denied ever having known Jesus.
- During all of chapter 23—the narratives of Jesus' trial, conviction, crucifixion, and burial—the disciples are conspicuous by their absence. There is mention of some women followers, and Joseph of Arimathea is the one who claims Jesus' body and is responsible for his burial. But there is no mention of the twelve.

- The disciples reappear in chapter 24. On the first day of the week the women returned from the tomb after having gone with the proper spices to prepare Jesus' body according to their custom. They discovered the tomb empty and returned with the news to the disciples. The report of the women seemed to be an "idle tale" but Peter ran to the tomb to confirm the women's story or to disprove it.
- Two disciples were walking to Emmaus when a third person joined them. They did not know that it was Jesus. The third person joined them for a meal and when he blessed and broke the bread "their eyes were opened and they recognized him." The two returned immediately to report their experience to the others.
- The disciples gathered in Jerusalem received the report of the two, and while they were together Jesus appeared in their midst. He showed them his wounds, ate with them, and then "he opened their minds to understand the scriptures." Jesus commissioned the disciples to share the good news of repentance and forgiveness of sins to all nations. Then, at Bethany Jesus blessed the disciples and departed from their midst.

These eleven scenes involving the disciples are very symbolic of the ways his followers respond to him today. We gather at table with our Lord and hardly understand the significance of what is happening. We are quick to promise our loyalty to Jesus and we just as quickly turn our backs on him. We have a hard time staying awake and focused when times become difficult, and we too need to be awakened by Jesus. We disappear when the going gets tough and there might be some risk or danger if we were to show our commitment to Jesus our Christ. We often do not recognize Jesus when he is right beside us. And then there are times when our eyes are opened because the truth of God's Word has been revealed to us. We, like the disciples, are quick to disbelieve the reports of others when those reports do not make any sense to us. And we are surprised and empowered when Jesus does become a part of our lives.

Three Themes in the Gospel of Luke

A whole chapter could be devoted to exploring the many themes that are prominent in the Gospel of Luke. All we will be able to do in this brief presentation is to identify three particular themes and provide a list of passages that represent each of them. You could follow up with each of these themes by reflecting on the passages and topics that are mentioned for each.

1. God's love is inclusive

Throughout the Gospel of Luke we read examples of Jesus reaching out to and including people from many different groups, many of whom were excluded by the faithful religious people of the day. In his "inaugural sermon" in Nazareth, Jesus stated the purpose of his ministry by quoting from the prophet Isaiah "to bring good news to the poor . . . proclaim release to the captives, and recovery of sight to the blind, to let the oppressed go free" (Luke 4:18). He then cited the examples from Elijah and Elisha ministering to a widow of Sidon and to a leper from Syria, both of whom are not among "the chosen ones." Jesus' declaration of this degree of inclusiveness offended the people and got him into trouble from the beginning of his ministry. It appears that Jesus offered God's love to all people no matter their status or station in life just because they are worthy of God's love and care. Some representative samples include the following:

- Tax collectors and sinners
  Eating with tax collectors and sinners (5:30)
  Encounter with Zacchaeus (9:1–10)
- Enemies
  Parable of the Good Samaritan (10:29–37)
  Love your enemies (6:27, 35)
- Women
  Women accompany Jesus on his journey (8:1–3)
  Jesus visits Mary and Martha (10:38–42)
  Poor widow with two coins (21:1–4)
  Women observe where Jesus is buried (23:55–56)
  Women are the first to see the empty tomb (24:1–12)
- The poor
  Jesus is to bring good news to the poor (4:18)
  "Blessed are you who are poor" (6:20)
  "When you give a banquet, invite the poor" (14:13)
  "Sell all that you own and distribute the money to the poor" (18:22)
- Children
  "Whoever welcomes this child in my name welcomes me" (9:48)
  "Let the little children come to me" (18:16–17)

2. Jesus at times of solitude and prayer

There are a number of occasions in Luke, more than in any of the other Gospels, where Jesus seeks solitude. The crowds often press upon him, and it is understandable that he would want to withdraw from them for a time of renewal and refreshment for his body and spirit. In Luke, on all of the occasions where Jesus draws apart from the crowds, and sometimes even from his disciples, the time of prayer and solitude precedes some significant action or decision. We could learn much from Jesus' way of coming close to God in prayer prior to making important decisions or engaging in critical events. Read some or all of the following passages and as you read consider several questions: 1. What prompted Jesus to spend the time in solitude? 2. What connections do you see between the time spent in solitude and what preceded and/or followed that time? 3. What can you learn from the example of Jesus spending time in solitude?

- Jesus was tempted in the wilderness (before beginning his ministry) (4:1–13)
- Jesus went to a lonely place (before going to other cities) (4:42–44)
- Jesus was praying in a lonely place (after cleansing a leper) (5:12–16)
- Jesus spent the whole night in prayer (before naming the twelve) (6:12–16)
- Jesus was praying alone (before Peter's confession of him as Messiah) (9:18–20)
- The appearance of his face changed (the transfiguration) (9:28–36)
- Jesus was praying in a certain place (and teaching the disciples the Lord's Prayer) (11:1–4)
- Jesus spent the night on the Mount of Olives (after entering Jerusalem) (21:34–38)
- Jesus prayed on the Mount of Olives (after the Passover meal) (22:39–46)

3. Jesus shares many meals

Another prominent theme in Luke is that a majority of his encounters with others are in conjunction with a meal. Jesus shares meals with tax collectors and sinners, with Pharisees, with women, and with his disciples. The many meal scenes in this Gospel suggest that this was a very important setting for the writer to communicate the essence of Jesus' ministry. "Here then is the heart of Luke's Gospel; after investigating everything carefully (1:3), the writer has found that he recognizes 'the truth concerning things about which we have been instructed' when memory of the actions and teachings of Jesus' ministry is enlightened by the Scriptures and reenacted in the hospitality and table fellowship of the community of believers."[1]

The following are representative occasions where Jesus shared a meal of significance with others. As you read some or all of these passages, notice several things: 1. With whom is Jesus sharing the meal? 2. What is the occasion of the meal? 3. What is the significance of the meal? 4. What happens after the meal?

- With Levi after calling him to be a disciple (5:27–32)
- With Simon the Pharisee (7:36–50)
- With five thousand hungry people (9:10–17)
- "Give us each day our daily bread" (11:3)
- Eating in the kingdom of God (13:22–30)
- With a leader of the Pharisees on the Sabbath (14:1–6)
- Parable of the Great Banquet (14:15–24)
- Celebration on the return of the Prodigal Son (15:11–32)
- The Passover meal with the disciples (22:14–23)
- Jesus is recognized in the breaking of the bread on the way to Emmaus (24:13–31)

1. From *New Interpreter's Bible,* vol. 9, *Luke and John,* R. Alan Culpepper (Nashville: Abingdon Press, 1995), 26.

Chapter Five
The Gospel of John

The Gospel of John is traditionally referred to as the Fourth Gospel. From very early times tradition held that the apostle John wrote this Fourth Gospel, as well as the three Epistles of John and the book of Revelation. However, as biblical scholars have carefully studied the language, style, and content of each of the books the majority concludes that John did not write these five books and that the author of the Fourth Gospel remains unknown. It is believed that this Gospel was written in the late first century, after the destruction of the Temple by the Romans in 70 CE.

Prayer Prompted by Scripture

One of the unique features of the Gospel of John is the six passages where Jesus identifies himself by a statement beginning, "I am . . ." This reminds us of the passage in Exodus where Moses experienced the revelation of God in a burning bush in the Midian desert. God called Moses to be the one to lead the Hebrews from the oppression of their slavery in Egypt. It is an understatement to say that Moses was reluctant to respond to God's call. He had several excuses and needed to be reassured by God several times. After declaring himself unworthy and being assured by God, "I will be with you," Moses had a second excuse of not knowing the name of God. God responded to Moses with the words, "I AM WHO I AM. . . . Thus you shall say to the Israelites, 'I AM has sent me to you'" (Exod. 3:14). The footnote associated with this holy name for God suggests that it can also be translated as, "I AM WHAT I AM" or "I WILL BE WHAT I WILL BE." The original Hebrew word, YHWH, is the divine name for God and is connected to the root verb meaning "to be." "I AM WHO I AM" is the essence of God's being.

The Gospel of John contains six different passages where Jesus identifies himself as embodying essential aspects of the natural and spiritual realms. He speaks of himself as the bread of life; the light of the world; the good shepherd; the resurrection and the life; the way, the truth, and the life; and the true vine. For our Prayer Prompted by Scripture, you will read the quotes from the Gospel and then pray a brief prayer responding to each saying.

Jesus said, "I am the bread of life" (John 6:35).
Feed me, O God, with the manna from heaven that nourishes my soul.
Jesus said, "I am the light of the world" (John 8:12).
Dear God, may the light of Jesus shine in the dark places of my life.
Jesus said, "I am the good shepherd" (John 10:11).
I thank you, dear God, for directing and correcting me with steadfast love.
Jesus said, "I am the resurrection and the life" (John 11:25).
I praise you God, for Jesus' victory over death and sin that is my victory as well.
Jesus said, "I am the way, and the truth, and the life" (John 14:6).
Help me to follow in the way of Christ, obedient to his truth and faithful to him.
Jesus said, "I am the true vine" (John 15:1).
O God, how wonderful it is to know that I am intimately bound to you forever.
Amen!

"Echoes" from the Hebrew Scriptures in the Gospel of John

Clearly, Jesus was thoroughly schooled in and knowledgeable of the Scriptures of his day, which we know as the Old Testament in our Bibles. It seems to me that Jesus and/or the writer were quite intentional in making connections or illusions to familiar concepts and images in the Hebrew Scriptures. Several of the "I am . . ." passages have explicit or implicit connections with one or more portions of the Hebrew Scriptures. It is almost as if we read and hear in Jesus' words an "echo" from familiar words in the Old Testament. I use the word "echo" to suggest that even though they may not be direct quotes, images and concepts reappear in the Gospel that remind us of what we see and hear in the Old Testament.

- "Bread of life": When I read of Jesus speaking of himself as the "bread of life" the image that comes to mind is the manna in the wilderness provided by God to satisfy the hunger of the Israelites during their desert journey (Exod. 16).

- "Light of the world": In the creation narrative we read, "Then God said, 'Let there be light'; and there was light. And God saw that the light was good; and God separated the light from the darkness" (Gen. 1:3–4).
- "Good shepherd": Two passages from the Hebrew Scriptures come immediately to mind: Psalm 23, "The Lord is my shepherd," and in Ezekiel where the prophet writes, "You are my sheep, the sheep of my pasture and I am your God, says the Lord GOD" (Ezek. 34:31).
- "The way, and the truth, and the life": We read in several psalms about the way and the truth, for example, "Teach me your way, O LORD, that I may walk in your truth" (Ps. 86:11). Also, "Happy are those whose way is blameless" and "O that my ways may be steadfast in keeping your statutes" (Ps. 119:1, 5).
- "The true vine": In Isaiah 5:1–6 the people of Israel are compared to a vineyard planted by God that did not yield good fruit and was destroyed. In Psalm 80:8, Isaiah 27:2–6, and Ezekiel 15:1–8 and 19:10–14 the image of a vineyard is used to speak about God as the keeper of the vineyard and the people of Israel as a vineyard planted, tended, pruned, and harvested by God.

The prologue of the Fourth Gospel (1:1–18) is another instance where there is an "echo" of a familiar passage from the Old Testament. Unlike Matthew and Luke, who include birth narratives at the beginning of their Gospels, John begins by connecting Jesus, the Word, with creation. "In the beginning was the Word, and the Word was with God, and the Word was God. . . . And the Word became flesh and lived among us, and we have seen his glory, the glory as of a father's only son, full of grace and truth" (1:1, 14). Take time to read Genesis 1:1–31 and then read John 1:1–18. As you read, notice how many images and concepts resonate between the two passages.

An Overview of the Gospel of John

The following overview of the Fourth Gospel is based on the outline of Gail R. O'Day in the *New Interpreter's Bible*, volume 9, *The Gospel of John.*

1. The prelude to Jesus' ministry (1:1–51)

Chapter 1 serves as an introduction to the whole Gospel. Verses 1–18 are identified as the prologue to the Gospel where the author presents Jesus as "The Word." The second part of the first chapter sets the stage for Jesus' ministry by introducing John the Baptist as the one who is preparing the way for the coming of the Messiah, and it also introduces the first of the disciples: Andrew, Simon, Nathaniel, and Philip.

2. Miracles and discourses (2:1–5:47)

This section begins with a wedding in Cana where Jesus performed the miracle of turning water into wine, then moves to Jerusalem where Jesus drove the money changers from the Temple. Jesus met a Pharisee, Nicodemus, and there is a long discourse about being born of water and spirit as compared to being born of the flesh. One of the most familiar verses in the Bible is a part of this encounter with Nicodemus: "For God so loved the world that he gave his only Son, so that everyone who believes in him may not perish but may have eternal life" (3:16). Jesus and his disciples returned to Galilee by way of Samaria. Another long discourse took place between Jesus and a woman of Samaria, the discussion focused on living water and worshiping God in spirit and in truth. The woman was the means by which a whole town came to believe in Jesus as the Savior of the world. Jesus returned to Cana, where he healed a royal official's son. This section ends with Jesus' return to Jerusalem, where on the sabbath he healed a man who had been ill for thirty-eight years. This act of Jesus provoked a controversy with the religious authorities because they believed Jesus had violated the Sabbath laws. This is followed by a discourse about the relationship between the Son (Jesus) and the Father (God).

3. A feeding miracle, discourses, and conflicts (6:1–10:42)

Jesus and his followers trek back to Galilee where a large crowd of people kept following Jesus. What follows is the miracle of the feeding of five thousand with five barley loaves and two fish that Andrew discovered in the lunch of a young boy. After this miracle there is a long discourse focused on Jesus' words, "I am the bread of life." Jesus alludes to drinking his blood and eating his flesh, which the disciples did not understand. The section ends with Jesus' declaration that one of the twelve would betray him.

Jesus was hesitant to go to Jerusalem for the festival of Booths but eventually did go. What began as a secret visit turned out to be very public, with Jesus teaching in the temple. Responses to his teaching were mixed. Some thought he was a prophet, others suspected he might have a demon, and some thought he might be the expected Messiah. There is a long discussion about the relationship between Abraham, the believers, and Jesus. Jesus healed a man who had been blind from birth, and this resulted in a dispute with the Jews as to whether the man was really blind. Jesus spoke of himself as the "gate for the sheep" and as "the good shepherd." The section ends with the religious authorities seeking to arrest Jesus.

4. A prelude to Jesus' hour (11:1–12:50)

Jesus went to Bethany to visit his friends, Mary, Martha, and Lazarus. He was informed that his dear friend, Lazarus, had died. Jesus responded that he was not dead but asleep. The remaining verses of chapter 11 tell of Lazarus being brought back to life after three days in a tomb and of the conflict that this caused among the Jewish authorities. They tried to arrest Jesus but he escaped. The account of Lazarus's coming back to life is a precursor of Jesus' own death and resurrection. Chapter 12 continues with Jesus' entry into Jerusalem and concludes with Jesus saying, "The hour has come for the Son of Man to be glorified"(12:23) and then interpreting the meaning of his death.

5. The farewell meal, discourse, and prayer (13:1–17:26)

Jesus prepared himself and his followers for his final hours with a last meal highlighted by his washing their feet to teach them about being servants of one another: "I give you a new commandment, that you love one another. Just as I have loved you, you also should love one another. By this everyone will know that you are my disciples, if you have love for one another" (13:34–35). Chapters 14 to 16 contain a series of long discourses, and chapter 17 is a long prayer of Jesus for himself and for his followers.

6. Jesus' arrest, trial, and death (18:1–19:42)

Jesus was in the garden with his disciples, all except Judas. The soldiers guided by Judas came to the garden to arrest Jesus. They took him first to Annas to be interrogated and then to Pilate. During this time Peter denied Jesus three times. There is an extended exchange between Pilate and Jesus. Pilate found no fault in him and desired to release him. The crowds, however, demanded that Jesus be crucified. Jesus was crucified on Golgotha while his mother and other women observed from a distance. After he died, Jesus' body was taken by Joseph of Arimathea and Nicodemus to be prepared for burial and then placed in a nearby tomb.

7. The first resurrection appearances of Jesus (20:1–31)

On the first day of the week Mary Magdalene went to the tomb and discovered the stone was removed from the entrance. She told Peter and one other disciple. They went to the tomb and discovered the body was missing, though the burial cloths remained. The disciples returned to their homes, but Mary stayed in the garden. There she encountered the risen Jesus. She told the disciples, and that evening Jesus appeared in their midst and they all believed. Thomas was not with them and he would not believe their word of Jesus' return. A week later Jesus appeared again when Thomas was present, and this time he believed.

8. Jesus' final resurrection appearance (21:1–25)

The disciples had returned to fishing but on that night they caught nothing. Jesus was on the shore as they were coming in and he told them to cast their nets on the other side of the boat, after which they filled their nets. They recognized Jesus with the words, "It is the Lord!" After sharing a meal together the final scene is an exchange between Jesus and Peter. Jesus asks Peter three times, "Simon, son of John, do you love me?" Three times Peter responds, "Yes, Lord; you know that I love you." And, each time Jesus says to Peter, "Feed (or tend) my lambs (or sheep)." Peter had denied Jesus three times, and now their relationship is restored as he promises to love and serve Jesus.

Differences between the Fourth Gospel and the Synoptics

In the previous three chapters we discovered that Matthew, Mark, and Luke have many parallel passages and are identified as the Synoptic Gospels, which means that they "see the gospel story together." Though they have much in common, each has particular characteristics that set it apart from the other two. When we turn to the Gospel of John we discover it to be very different from the other three. Some of the differences between John and the other three Gospels include the following.

More theological

The author of the Fourth Gospel presents several theological concepts that are not as fully developed in the other three Gospels. The *incarnation* (God appearing in the flesh) is introduced in the prologue (1:1–18) of the Gospel and is developed further in Jesus' discourse about his relationship with the Father: "Whoever has seen me has seen the Father. How can you say, 'Show us the Father?' Do you not believe that I am in the Father and the Father is in me?" (14:9–10). The author presents a clear understanding of *salvation* and *eternal life*. "For God so loved the world that he gave his only Son, so that everyone who believes in him may not perish but may have eternal life" (3:16). And, in 5:24 we read, "Very truly, I tell you, everyone who hears my word and believes him who sent me has eternal life." This Gospel also presents a doctrine of the *Spirit*. In his discussion with Nicodemus, Jesus speaks about being born of the Spirit. We also read, "And I will ask the Father, and he will give you another Advocate, to be with you forever. This is the Spirit of truth" (14:16–17). In his appearance among the disciples after the resurrection "[Jesus] breathed on them and said to them, 'Receive the Holy Spirit'" (20:22).

Long discourses

As you skim through the whole Gospel or review the outline of the Gospel in the previous section you will notice many long discourses of Jesus. The discourses are in the context of encounters with individuals (Nicodemus and the Samaritan woman), with his disciples, with the crowds when he was teaching in the temple, with the authorities during his trials, and with his Father as in the great prayer in chapter 17.

Different recording of events

In the other three Gospels, Jesus spends most of his time in Galilee and goes to Jerusalem only in the final days of his ministry. In the Fourth Gospel, Jesus moves back and forth between Galilee and Judea and Jerusalem (2:13; 5:1; 7:10). Three Passovers are mentioned in John where Jesus goes to Jerusalem (2:13; 6:4; 12:12). In the Synoptics, Jesus cleanses the temple after his entry into Jerusalem at the beginning of his last week, whereas in John the cleansing occurred on his first trip to the city. In the Gospel of John there is no "last supper" where Jesus calls attention to the bread and wine as being his body and blood, as in the other three. Instead the final Passover meal with Jesus features the foot washing and Jesus teaching about servanthood. The events surrounding the crucifixion and resurrection are presented differently in John than in the other three Gospels.

Fewer miracles

The Fourth Gospel has fewer miracles (nine) performed by Jesus than in the other three Gospels (Matthew, twenty; Mark and Luke, nineteen each). Only one miracle of Jesus is recorded in all four of the Gospels, the feeding of the five thousand. Moreover, in John miracles are often referred to as *signs* (2:11, 20:30).

No parables

There are no parables in John's Gospel. On the other hand, there are many parables in each of the other Gospels (Matthew, twenty-one; Mark, eight; Luke, twenty-five). It is clear that Jesus' teaching in John was more in the context of discourses, and in the other Gospels the method of Jesus' teaching was through the use of parables.

Two key persons

Two major narratives with discourses appear in the Gospel of John that are not mentioned at all in the other three Gospels. The encounters and discussions with Nicodemus (3:1–21) and with the Samaritan woman (4:1–42) are pivotal stories in this Gospel and serve to communicate important truths about "being born of the Spirit" and Jesus being the "living water."

Names and Titles of Jesus

In the Gospel of John, as in the other Gospels, many names, titles, and images are used to identify Jesus. It is clear that there is no one name, title, or image that is sufficient to identify this person who is so unique and mysterious. The people in the crowds, the disciples, and those who oppose Jesus all name him in different ways. Jesus also identifies himself by six different images. Let's review briefly the most common names, titles, and images for Jesus in the Gospel of John.

Jesus

The writer of the Fourth Gospel uses the name Jesus approximately 250 times. Jesus is derived from the Hebrew "Joshua" and means "God saves." Others address Jesus or speak about him using other designations.

Word

The Gospel opens with the words, "In the beginning was the Word, and the Word was with God, and the Word was God" (1:1). The Greek word for Word is *logos*. This word and concept are familiar to both Greeks and Jews. Jesus is seen both as existing at the dawn of creation, attesting to his deity, and also as "the Word became flesh," revealing his humanity. This is one of the most challenging passages in the Gospel, if not in the whole New Testament. Nowhere else in the Gospels does this name for Jesus appear and elsewhere in the New Testament only in Revelation (19:13).

Lamb of God

In 1:29 and 36, Jesus is identified as the "Lamb of God" by John the Baptist, who associates Jesus with the Passover lamb. Passover was the festival celebration of the deliverance of the people of Israel from bondage in Egypt. The blood of a lamb was placed on the doorposts of the homes of the Hebrew slaves. Jesus is (or will be) the sacrificial lamb during the Passover festival later in his ministry. These two verses are the only places in the Gospels where Jesus is named as the Lamb of God.

Rabbi

Jesus is identified as "Rabbi," which means teacher, more often (eight times) than by any other title. His disciples call him "Rabbi" (4:31; 9:2; 11:7), as did the crowd (6:25). In addition, John the Baptist's disciples (1:38), Nathaniel (1:49), Nicodemus (3:2), and Mary Magdalene, when she experienced the risen Christ (20:16), all address Jesus as "Rabbi." The terms *rabbi*, *teacher*, and *master* all have the same connotation and are the most frequently used titles for Jesus in all of the Gospels.

Messiah

The Hebrew word for "messiah" means "anointed one." The prophets of the Hebrew Scriptures expressed anticipation that God would send a Messiah to free the people of Israel from persecution, sin, and death. He would usher in a new day of deliverance with peace, justice, and hope prevailing. Some expected the Messiah would come with a military victory, defeating all of the forces of evil and oppression. The prophet Isaiah offered an image of the Messiah as a Suffering Servant. Simon Peter is among the first to see Jesus as Messiah (1:41). In her encounter with Jesus at Jacob's well, a Samaritan woman speaks of Messiah, and he says, "I am he, the one who is speaking to you" (4:25–26). In John chapter 7 the word "Messiah" appears six times. The people debated whether Jesus was the Messiah; some believed and others doubted. Jesus was part of the debate but does not declare that he is the Messiah. Later, Jesus is asked by some of the Jews, "How long will you keep us in suspense? If you are the Messiah, tell us plainly." Jesus answered, "I have told you, and you do not believe" (10:24–25). The author of the Gospel concludes chapter 20 with the words, "These are written so that you may come to believe that Jesus is the

Messiah, the Son of God, and that through believing you may have life in his name" (20:30). The Hebrew word for "messiah" is translated in the Greek as "Christ."

Savior

In only one place in the Gospel is Jesus referred to as "savior." The Samaritan woman, after coming to know Jesus as the Messiah, returned to her village to tell all of her experience with Jesus. The people believed her and invited Jesus to stay with them, which he did for two days. After his visit the people said to the woman, "It is no longer because of what you said that we believe, for we have heard for ourselves, and we know that this is truly the Savior of the world" (4:42).

Son of Joseph and Jesus of Nazareth

These two designations for Jesus identify his connections to a specific family and a specific location, as was customary in the time Jesus lived. Jesus called Philip to follow him and then Philip found Nathaniel to tell him about Jesus. He spoke of Jesus as "son of Joseph from Nazareth" (1:45). Nathaniel wonders if any good thing can come from Nazareth; but, after meeting Jesus he made his own confession, "Rabbi, you are the Son of God! You are the King of Israel!" (1:49). At the time of his arrest in the garden, the soldiers came looking for Jesus of Nazareth, and Jesus replied, "I am he" (18:5). After Jesus' arrest, trial, and conviction, Pilate ordered a sign made to hang over Jesus' head on the cross. It read, "Jesus of Nazareth, the King of the Jews" (19:19).

King

The title of "king" is used in reference to Jesus thirteen times in the Gospel. Nathaniel spoke of Jesus as "King of Israel" (1:49) as did the people who applauded Jesus' entrance into Jerusalem shouting, "Hosanna! Blessed is the one who comes in the name of the Lord—the King of Israel!" (12:13). Early in his ministry, after the miracle of loaves and fishes, Jesus realized the people wanted to "make him king" so he escaped to a remote place on the mountain to be by himself (6:15.) Most of the other references to Jesus as king are spoken at the time of his trial by Pilate, who tries to get Jesus to admit that he is the King of Jews, which Jesus refused to do. The soldiers mocked Jesus by calling him "King of the Jews" as they slapped him on the face (19:3).

Lord

There are thirty-five verses where Jesus is addressed as "Lord" and in each instance it is only the disciples, close friends, and one who is healed by Jesus who call him "Lord." Mary Magdalene was the first to recognize Jesus after his resurrection, and when she went to report her good news to the disciples she said, "I have seen the Lord" (20:18). The apostle Thomas was not present when Jesus appeared to the disciples on the day of his resurrection and he would not believe. A week later Jesus appeared again and Thomas was present. After confirming Jesus was truly alive he declared, "My Lord and my God" (20:28).

Chapter Six
The Acts of the Apostles

The book of Acts is unique in the New Testament. It is the second volume by the author whom tradition identified as Luke. This volume continues the story of God's great and wonderful acts through the followers of Jesus Christ, the One whom they proclaimed as God's Messiah. All of the other books of the New Testament are either Gospels or Epistles, with the exception of Revelation. Acts is often thought of as a book of history of the first-century church. True, many key events and persons are presented in a chronological fashion. However, the book is an unfolding of a theological narrative that summarizes much of what the earliest Christians believed as they developed a unique identity as the Church of Jesus Christ. The book includes sermons, speeches, biographical sketches, theological debates, and travelogues. Acts was written after the Gospel of Luke, perhaps between 80 and 90 CE. The author continues the story from the first volume, which ended with Jesus' ascension into the heavens while he and the disciples were together in Bethany.

We should spend several chapters on the book of Acts in order to do it proper justice. However, we have just this one chapter to try to gain a sense of the essence of the book. After the following Prayer Prompted by Scripture, we focus our attention on an overview of the book, a review of the growth and development of the early church as it moved beyond Jerusalem, and a summary of three major themes.

Prayer Prompted by Scripture

In the previous four chapters we read many passages from the four Gospels where Jesus called his followers into a life of discipleship and mission. The following prayer follows a pattern that we have used before where a saying of Jesus is quoted and is followed by a brief prayer. Read the following seven passages and reflect on them prayerfully as you read/pray the brief responses. If you have time, you may express your own prayer responses by writing or praying silently.

Jesus said, "Follow me" (Mark 2:14).
O God, help me to hear your call and inspire me to respond in faith.
Jesus said, "The harvest is plentiful, but the laborers are few" (Matt. 9:37).
Truly there is much work to do to share your Good News. Equip me, O God, to be among those laborers willing to do your work.
Jesus said, "A disciple is not above the teacher . . . it is enough for the disciple to be like the teacher" (Matt. 10:24–25).
In the face of all you want me to be and do I feel overwhelmed and inadequate; may I know your presence and power in my life.
Jesus said, "Whoever welcomes you welcomes me, and whoever welcomes me welcomes the one who sent me" (Matt. 10:40).
Lord God, may I be friendly and caring toward others so that I will be received as one who reflects Jesus' love, compassion, and forgiveness.
Jesus said, "You did not choose me but I chose you. And I appointed you to go and bear fruit" (John 15:16).
It is a mystery why you have chosen me to be one of your disciples. Help me to follow Jesus faithfully so that I may bear much good fruit.
Jesus said, "By this everyone will know that you are my disciples, if you have love for one another" (John 13:35).
It is hard to love everyone and treat them as children of God. May I be blessed with the will and the ability to love others the way Jesus loves them.
Jesus said, "Go therefore and make disciples of all nations, baptizing them . . . and teaching them to obey everything that I have commanded you. And remember, I am with you always, to the end of the age" (Matt. 28:19–20).
That is a tremendous task and responsibility, dear God. Give me the strength and the courage to fulfill Jesus' command, knowing he is with me each day.

An Overview of the Acts of the Apostles

There are many parts to the narrative presented in the Acts of the Apostles. Each part is filled with situations, events, and persons that reveal God's Spirit at work in the midst of the first believers to spread the good news of the gospel of Jesus Christ and to form a viable movement that became the Christian church, the body of Christ. As I review this book there appear to be eleven distinct sections, which are briefly described below.

1. Jesus' last words and ascension (1:1–11)

The author continues where he left off in volume one, the Gospel of Luke. Jesus is present with his disciples. He promises them that they will receive power from the Holy Spirit to be his "witnesses in Jerusalem, in all Judea and Samaria, and to the ends of the earth" (1:8). This promise and command of Jesus sets the stage for the unfolding of the whole narrative that follows.

2. Matthias chosen to replace Judas (1:12–26)

The criteria for choosing a successor to Judas were that the person would have been present during Jesus' ministry and would have been a witness to the resurrection. Two candidates were presented, and after much prayer and casting lots, Matthias was chosen.

3. The day of Pentecost: The church is born (2:1–47)

The disciples were gathered together for the traditional Pentecost festival and, as promised, they experienced the gift of the Holy Spirit symbolized by the rush of a great wind and tongues of fire. They shared their gift with others who were present from many countries, Peter preached his first sermon, and three thousand people believed and were baptized. Thus, the Christian church was born.

4. The believers in Jerusalem (3:1–7:60)

The activity of the first days of the new community of believers involved healing people, sharing possessions, proclaiming the good news, defending their faith, praying and worshiping, setting standards, and getting organized. Seven men "of good standing, full of the Spirit and of wisdom" were selected as the first deacons to respond to the needs of widows and others. Stephen was chosen as one of the seven. Later, Stephen was charged with blasphemy because of his faithful witness. Chapter 7 includes his speech in defense of his faith and concludes with him being stoned to death. His last words are reported to have been, "Lord Jesus, receive my spirit . . . do not hold this sin against them" (7:59–60), which sound very much like Jesus' words of forgiveness from the cross.

5. The gospel spreads beyond Jerusalem (8:1–12:24)

This section begins with reports of the activities of Saul persecuting the Christians and Philip preaching in Samaria and witnessing to an Ethiopian official. Chapter 9 tells of Saul's conversion and his acceptance by the disciples in a dramatic meeting in Jerusalem. The narrative continues with Peter as a key person in presenting the good news to Gentiles. He is able to convince the apostles in Jerusalem that it was God's will that Gentiles be baptized and welcomed into the community because they also had received the gift of the Holy Spirit. The church continued to grow with a strong faith community in Antioch, where the believers were for the first time called "Christians." This section concludes with reports of King Herod's persecution of Christians, the killing of the apostle James, and the imprisonment of Peter.

6. The first missionary journey (13:1–14:28)

Saul and Barnabas are commissioned by the church in Antioch to go on a journey to proclaim the good news. This section includes accounts of their many adventures on the Island of Cyprus and in several cities on the mainland of Asia Minor. Usually, they first met with the Jewish community in the synagogue where they would preach the good news of Jesus as the Messiah. Read 13:13–50 as an example of the message they preached and the typical reaction of the people to the preaching. The section concludes with their return to Antioch where Paul and Barnabas report all that God had done and how "he had opened a door of faith for the Gentiles" (14:27).

7. The council at Jerusalem (15:1–35)

A dispute arose among the leaders of the young church as to whether Gentile converts were to be subject to the same ritual laws as the Jews, particularly the matter of circumcision. The apostles and elders gathered in Jerusalem to consider the matter. After they heard testimony from Paul and Barnabas, the leaders decided that such a ritual should not be required of the Gentile believers. A letter was sent informing the church in Antioch of this decision.

8. The second missionary journey (15:36–18:22)

Paul invited Barnabas to make a return visit to the believers in the places where they had proclaimed the good news, but Barnabas declined because Paul was unwilling to have John Mark, Barnabas's nephew, accompany them because he had left them on the previous journey. Instead, Paul chose Silas to join him for this journey. Barnabas and John Mark sailed to Cyprus while Paul and Silas went overland to Derbe, Lystra, the region of Galatia, on to Troas. Paul had a vision of a man pleading for him to bring the good news to Macedonia. They went to Macedonia, where Paul and Silas preached and then were placed in prison. After their release they moved on to Thessalonica, Beroea, Athens, and Corinth. In every community were people who believed and were baptized as well as those who objected to Paul's message of Jesus as the Messiah. Paul was joined by Barnabas and Timothy in Corinth, where they stayed for eighteen months before returning to Syria. On their way they made a stop in Ephesus and promised they would return.

9. The third missionary journey (18:23–21:8)

There is no indication how much time elapsed between the second and third journeys. Leaving Antioch, Paul retraced much of his previous journey by visiting Ephesus, Troas, Macedonia, and Greece. His message was the cause of a riot in Ephesus. After his visit to Greece and Macedonia, Paul returned to Ephesus for a farewell visit before he sailed back to Tyre in Syria.

10. Paul in Jerusalem (21:9–26:32)

Even though Paul was warned not to go to Jerusalem, he was determined to go. Paul is quoted, "For I am ready not only to be bound but even to die in Jerusalem for the name of the Lord Jesus" (21:13b). His friends replied, "The Lord's will be done." Paul visited the elders in Jerusalem to report the results of his journey. While he was teaching in the temple, the crowd was incited against Paul with the words, "Fellow Israelites, help! This is the man who is teaching everyone everywhere against our people, our law, and this place" (21:28). Chapters 25 and 26 present a dramatic series of encounters between Paul and the Roman authorities wherein he made a very persuasive defense of his cause. He appealed to the emperor of Rome for his case to be resolved there instead of in Jerusalem. Read chapter 26 to learn about Paul's life as he tells the story of his youth, his conversion, and his ministry in Jesus' name, making his defense before King Agrippa. He even invited the king to believe in Jesus. The king is persuaded that Paul is innocent, but since he appealed his case to the emperor he must be sent to Rome.

11. The journey to Rome (27:1–28:31)

The account of Paul's voyage to Rome is amazing for all of its detail. There are details regarding navigation and seamanship, the three ships that transported him, the weather conditions, the shipwreck, and Paul's leadership in the midst of the crises of the journey. As you read these two chapters, have a map in front of you so you can visualize the progress of the voyage. It is interesting that Paul began the journey as a prisoner under a centurion's custody and later became the one who convinced all on board the ship in the time of crisis to believe him and follow his orders. This segment of the story ends with Paul under house arrest in Rome for two years. The narrative ends without reporting what finally happened to Paul. Even while under house arrest he preached the good news of Jesus as the long-awaited Messiah. Some believed, whereas many refused to believe.

Thus ends the marvelous story of the gospel of Jesus Christ, whose following grew from a small band in Jerusalem to a scattering of believers in all the major towns and cities of the Roman empire. Men and women, free and slave, Jews and Gentiles are welcomed to the community of believers. By the time we get to chapter 28 we see that Jesus' promise and command of chapter 1 have been fulfilled: "You will receive power when the Holy Spirit has come upon you; and you will be my witnesses in Jerusalem, in all Judea and Samaria, and to the ends of the earth" (1:8).

A Spirit-Led Church

We began and ended the eleven sections of our outline by quoting Jesus' parting words about his followers receiving power when the Holy Spirit has come upon them. They must have wondered what Jesus meant, but they trusted him and they waited. They were together in an upper room in Jerusalem on the Day of Pentecost when Jesus' promise was fulfilled. Pentecost was a harvest festival of the Jews, first called the Festival of Weeks (Num. 28:26–31 and Deut. 16:9–12), which occurred fifty days after Passover. Jesus' followers were in Jerusalem, along with devout Jews from many countries, to celebrate the festival, according to their Jewish custom.

The account of them receiving the gift of the Holy Spirit is described as "the rush of a violent wind filling the entire house" and "tongues, as of fire, resting upon them." Wind and fire are powerful, rich symbols that are used to represent God's power and presence in many places in the Old and New Testaments. In the first day of creation "a wind from God swept over the face of the waters" (Gen. 1:2). In a footnote we discover that the Hebrew word translated as "wind," *ruach*, can also be translated as "breath" and "spirit." Psalm 104:4 reads that God makes "the winds [God's] messengers." In John's Gospel we read, "He breathed on them and said to them, 'Receive the Holy Spirit'" (John 20:22). Fire also is frequently used as a symbol to represent God's presence. Moses heard God call from a burning bush that was on fire but was not consumed (Exod. 3:2). During the exodus the people of Israel were led to the mountain of God by a pillar of cloud by day and fire by night (Exod. 13:21–22). The fire on the altar was to be kept burning to signify that God was present (Lev. 6:12–13). In the preaching of

John the Baptist, anticipating the ministry of Jesus, he says, "I baptize you with water for repentance, but one who is more powerful than I is coming after me; I am not worthy to carry his sandals. He will baptize you with the Holy Spirit and fire" (Matt. 3:11).

The gift of the Holy Spirit on that day was sufficient to give Jesus' followers the power and courage to tell everyone who would listen what had happened to them. The bystanders thought they were drunk. Peter dismissed that accusation and proceeded to preach a powerful sermon. As a result of that message, three thousand people repented of their sins and were baptized. The new community of believers was off to a great start.

It did not take long for the disciples to encounter opposition to their message. Peter and John were jailed. When they were released, they gathered with their friends and spent much time in prayer. As a result, "the place in which they were gathered together was shaken; and they were all filled with the Holy Spirit and spoke the word of God with boldness" (Acts 4:31). Stephen was filled with the Holy Spirit and given courage to speak the truth about Jesus despite the threat of death, which was the result of his testimony (7:55). While Peter was preaching, the Holy Spirit came to those who were listening, including the Gentiles (10:44–45). In Antioch, while the believers were worshiping, the Holy Spirit spoke to the gathered community: "Set apart for me Barnabas and Saul for the work to which I have called them" (13:2). In Paul's last words to the church in Ephesus as he departed, knowing he would not see them again, he said to them, "Keep watch over yourselves and over all the flock, of which the Holy Spirit has made you overseers, to shepherd the church of God that he obtained with the blood of his own Son" (20:28).

These few examples from Acts show how important the Holy Spirit was in providing the power, direction, and motivation for proclaiming Jesus as the Christ, the promised Messiah, for Jews and Gentiles alike. The Holy Spirit provided the power for healing, for repentance and baptism, for speaking the truth, for receiving Gentiles as well as Jews into the community of believers, for commissioning particular persons for special responsibilities, for guidance in making decisions when confronted by difficult issues, and for facing threats of persecution and death. A question for us to ask ourselves and our churches today is, "How and where is the Holy Spirit working among us and leading us?" Perhaps we need to rediscover more about the early church and how it listened to and was led by the Holy Spirit.

The Life and Work of the Infant Church

The passage immediately after reporting the conversion and baptism of three thousand believers on the Day of Pentecost reads, "They [the baptized ones] devoted themselves to the apostles' teaching and fellowship, to the breaking of bread and the prayers" (2:42). In this one verse we see four marks of the early church.

1. The church in its first days was a *teaching church.* The apostles were the first teachers and they taught the believers what they had learned from and experienced with Jesus, their Lord and Master. The meaning of the word *apostle* in Greek is "one sent out." They were sent out not only as witnesses of Jesus' teaching, but even more important, they were witnesses of the risen Christ.

2. The infant church was also one that experienced *fellowship* (in Greek, *koinonia*) with one another. Fellowship means more than enjoying the company of the gathered body. In this context, fellowship is the common bond the believers have with one another, not because they enjoy one another's company but because of the shared confession of faith they have made that Jesus Christ is their Lord. It is this fellowship of faith and commitment that formed the body of Christ, the church, and bound the believers to one another in life and in death.

3. The first believers were also a community that *broke bread together.* There are several connotations in this act of breaking bread. Bread is the symbol of what gives sustenance and life. One must eat bread in order to live. I suspect that some of the believers remembered Jesus saying, "I am the bread of life." Another aspect is that they shared common meals because some of their number were poor and did not have enough bread to eat. Later in the church's life, by the time the book of Acts was written, there was probably an association with breaking bread in the Lord's supper to remember Jesus' life, death, and resurrection.

4. The early Christians also were a *praying* church. A replacement for Judas was chosen after prayer. While believers were being persecuted, as an answer to the prayers of the believers God provided protection and patience. The Holy Spirit came into the lives of individuals and communities of believers while they were in a time and place of prayer.

When we read the whole book of Acts we discover many examples of the believers learning from the apostles' teaching, sharing meaningful fellowship, breaking bread together, and spending time in prayer.

The few verses following 2:42 also reveal much more about the life and work of the early church.

> Awe came upon everyone, because many wonders and signs were being done by the apostles. All who believed were together and had all things in common; they would sell their possessions and goods and distribute the proceeds to all, as any had need. Day by day, as they spent much time together in the temple, they broke bread at home and ate their food with glad and generous hearts, praising God and having the goodwill of all the people. And day by day the Lord added to their number those who were being saved. (Acts 2:43–47)

God was at work in amazing and powerful ways among this small community of believers. In Acts 17:6 they were called "These people who have been turning the world upside down." No doubt the energy they received and the empowerment they felt enabled them to do God's work of proclaiming the good news of new life for each day, hope for the future, and an everlasting faith. This was all available through commitment to Jesus the Christ, and it did turn the world upside down for many people, especially those in power and the custodians of the traditions. It was not just a matter of being satisfied by belonging to a community of fellow believers; it was very important to take the good news of Jesus the Christ to all who would listen, "to the ends of the earth."

A key line of the passage quoted above is, "And day by day the Lord added to their number those who were being saved." The believers joined together to become a teaching church, a church committed to Jesus Christ, a church celebrating in the breaking of bread, a worshiping and praying church, a serving church, and a church reaching out to all who would listen. And, because of the quality of their life together, the commitment to their Lord, and the motivation to witness to their faith, they became a growing church. Again, we can learn much from the church of the first century as we seek to be faithful to Jesus Christ in the twenty-first century.

Three Topics to Explore

At the beginning of this chapter we realized that there are so many persons, events, issues, and concepts presented in the book of Acts that we would only be able to scratch the surface of all the material it would be possible to explore. In order to avoid extending this chapter any more than it is, I present these suggested passages so that you can explore further three topics that may be of interest to you.

1. The spread of the good news beyond Jerusalem

In the first chapter of Acts we read that Jesus told his disciples they would receive power from the Holy Spirit in order to be his "witnesses in Jerusalem, in all Judea and Samaria, and to the ends of the earth" (1:8). Then, in the last chapter we see that Paul was in Rome, and for two years he proclaimed the good news of Jesus the Christ, the one promised by the prophets of old. With a map alongside your Bible, read the following passages.

- 1:6–8: Jesus' promise and command to be his witnesses.
- 2:1–13: Disciples and many devout Jews are gathered in Jerusalem.
- 8:1b–3: All except the disciples are scattered throughout Judea and Samaria.
- 8:4–8: Philip goes to Samaria to proclaim the Messiah to them.
- 8:26–40: Philip speaks of the good news of Jesus to an Ethiopian official.
- 9:19b–25: Saul preaches in Damascus.
- 10:1ff: Peter preaches to Gentiles in Joppa.
- 11:19–26: The church in Antioch.
- 13:1–14:28: First missionary journey to Cyprus and Asia Minor.
- 16:1–18:18: Second missionary journey to Galatia, Macedonia, and Greece.
- 19:1–21:16: Third missionary journey to Ephesus, Macedonia, and Greece.
- 27:1–28:31: The voyage to Rome.

There are several questions for you to consider as you read these passages.

Who were the persons involved?

What prompted the movement of the person(s) to travel to share the gospel?

What were the results of proclaiming the good news of Jesus the Christ?

2. Conversion experiences of crowds and individuals

The purpose of being witnesses of the good news of Jesus is so that persons will repent of their sins, receive the Holy Spirit and be baptized, and commit to a new way of living and believing. The power the disciples received from the Holy Spirit to be such witnesses produced many converts to the Way of Jesus.

- 2:14–42: Peter preaches on Pentecost and three thousand people are baptized.
- 3:11–3:4: Peter preaches and five thousand believe.
- 8:26–39: Philip shares the good news of Jesus; an Ethiopian official is baptized.
- 9:1–19a: Paul's conversion on the road to Damascus.
- 10:34–48: Gentiles receive the Holy Spirit after hearing Peter preach.
- 13:42–52: Many Gentiles in Pisidia believe after Paul and Barnabas preach.
- 16:11–15: Lydia, the first convert in Europe.
- 16:25–34: A Philippian jailer and his family believe.
- 18:1–8: A synagogue leader, his family, and others are baptized in Corinth.

Consider the following questions as you read these passages about conversion.

Who experiences the conversion?

Who serves as Jesus' witness to prompt the conversion?

What are the factors contributing to the conversion?

What are the results of the conversion?

3. Conflicts as a result of witnessing to the good news of Jesus as Messiah

It is no surprise that the apostles encountered opposition when they were so bold as to proclaim the good news of Jesus as the Messiah. They experienced this opposition from the Jews, the Romans, local officials, and even from their own members.

- 4:1–22: Peter and John in conflict with the elders and teachers of the law.
- 5:17–42: Peter and other apostles are arrested.
- 6:8–8:1a: Stephen accused of blasphemy and martyred for his beliefs.
- 9:26–30: Paul not trusted by the apostles at first.
- 11:1–18: Peter criticized for taking the good news to the Gentiles.
- 15:1–33: The Jerusalem Council deals with obligations of Gentiles to the law.
- 16:16–40: Paul and Silas are put in prison.
- 19:23–41: A riot in Ephesus.
- 22:30–26:32: Paul defends himself before various Roman officials.

As you read the passages, consider the following questions.

Who were the parties to the conflict?

What was the cause of the conflict?

How was the conflict resolved?

What was the role of the Holy Spirit in the conflict, if any?

Chapter Seven

Epistles of the New Testament

Our focus in this chapter is the collection of books in the New Testament that are identified as letters or epistles. There are twenty-one such books written by various authors and addressed to different individuals and groups in the context of real situations and issues. The apostle Paul wrote some of the letters to churches that he had visited. The authors of some of the letters are unknown. These epistles were written to communicate the gospel and to encourage the young churches to remain faithful in their commitment to Christ as their Lord and Savior.

Prayer Prompted by Scripture

One of the most familiar chapters in the whole New Testament is 1 Corinthians 13, the love chapter. Portions of the chapter are often read at weddings. It is also the subject of many sermons and Bible study lessons. We focus on this familiar chapter for our beginning prayer. You will read the passage from the Contemporary English Version of the Bible. You may be more familiar with the New Revised Standard Version or the King James Version of the passage. If so, reading the passage in a newer translation may prompt you to reflect on the words in a fresh way to gain added understanding. You may also want to read the passage in your own Bible, either in addition to or instead of reading it as printed below.

What if I could speak all languages of humans and angels?
If I did not love others,
I would be nothing more than a noisy gong or a clanging cymbal.
What if I could prophesy and understand all secrets and all knowledge?
And what if I had faith that moved mountains?
I would be nothing, unless I loved others.
What if I gave away all that I owned and let myself be burned alive?
I would gain nothing, unless I loved others.
Love is kind and patient, never jealous, boastful, proud, or rude.
Love isn't selfish or quick tempered.
It doesn't keep a record of wrongs that others do.
Love rejoices in the truth, but not in evil.
Love is always supportive, loyal, hopeful, and trusting.
Love never fails!
Everyone who prophesies will stop,
and unknown languages will no longer be spoken.
All that we know will be forgotten.
We don't know everything, and our prophecies are not complete.
But what is perfect will someday appear, and what isn't perfect will then disappear.
When we were children, we thought and reasoned as children do.
But when we grew up we quit our childish ways.
Now all we can see of God is like a cloudy picture in a mirror.
Later we will see him face to face.
We don't know everything, but then we will,
just as God completely understands us.
For now there are faith, hope, and love.
But of these three, the greatest is love.

After you have read 1 Corinthians 13, take a few minutes to reflect on the passage guided by these questions.

How many characteristics of love do you see in the passage?

What examples can you think of in Jesus' life and ministry that reflect these characteristics of love?

Which of the characteristics of love would you like to increase in your own life? Spend a few minutes praying to God to help you grow in this way.

What words will you pray to express your thanksgiving for the love you know in Jesus Christ and the love that is shown to you by your family and friends?

Epistles in the New Testament

The collection of letters is about one-third of the whole New Testament. It is not possible to do justice to this volume of material in one chapter. The best we can do is to introduce a few of the letters with a brief overview of each. We consider several aspects of each letter: the author, the readers to whom the letter was addressed, and some of the central teachings of the letter. It would take considerable time and effort to read all of the letters, or even the few representative letters featured in this chapter. You will find several suggested chapters to read that will help you gain a sense of some of the important content of each of the letters we explore. The epistles we review include Romans, 1 Corinthians, Galatians, Ephesians, and 1 and 2 Thessalonians.

Romans

Read 1:1–17 (greeting and prayer of thanksgiving); 5:1–11 (justified by faith); 8:1–39 (life in the Spirit); 11:1–24 (salvation for Jews and Gentiles); 12:1–21 (the new life in Christ); and 15:14–33 (Paul's reasons for writing and his plans to visit Rome).

Romans appears first in the list of the epistles, not because it was the first one written but more likely because of its prominence in the collection of epistles. It is the longest of all the letters and contains the best developed presentation of Paul's theology. Romans was probably one of the last of the letters to be written by Paul, sometime in the late 50s CE.

Paul states in chapter 15 that he desired to visit the Christians in Rome but first needed to return to Jerusalem to take with him a collection of money that he had raised on behalf of those who were impoverished in Jerusalem. We read in Acts of Paul's return to Jerusalem after his third journey after he had spent extended periods of time in Corinth and Ephesus, but there is no mention of taking an offering to the Christians at this time. Paul indicates that his next trip will take him to Rome on his way to Spain (15:24).

It is not known when the church in Rome was founded or by whom. By the time Paul writes the letter, however, there is a considerable Christian community composed of Jewish and Gentile converts. A significant part of the letter addresses questions regarding how the Jewish and Gentile Christians are related to each other, how they relate to God in the light of Jesus as Messiah, and how each should observe the traditional laws of Moses in light of the life and teachings of Jesus.

The greeting and prayer in 1:1–17 introduce the essence of the message Paul desires to communicate to the Christians in Rome. He introduces himself as a servant and apostle of Jesus Christ. He declares that Jesus is the promised Messiah, a descendent of David, born of the flesh; is the Son of God; by the Spirit was raised from the dead; and is one who brings salvation to Jews and Gentiles alike. Read Romans 11:1–24 for a more developed presentation of this subject.

A major theme of Paul's message to the church in Rome is summarized in 5:1: "Therefore, since we are justified by faith, we have peace with God through our Lord Jesus Christ." Christian believers, whether they are Jew or Gentile, cannot earn their way into a relationship with God either by obeying the law or by good works. It is only by the undeserved grace of God and faith in Jesus as Lord and Savior that one comes into relationship with God. Paul explores this theological point thoroughly and persuasively.

Chapter 8 begins with a comparison between life lived according to the flesh and life lived in the Spirit and moves to 8:26: "Likewise the Spirit helps us in our weakness." This chapter also testifies to Paul's abiding faith in God through Jesus Christ as he challenges all who read his words to share in that same faith. "We know that all things work together for good for those who love God" (8:28). "If God is for us, who is against us?" (8:31). "[Nothing] in all creation, will be able to separate us from the love of God in Christ Jesus our Lord" (8:39). These are very encouraging words for the Christians in Rome and also for us today. These words are worth memorizing and are worthy of our believing as we live day by day in a world that is often confusing, threatening, and dehumanizing.

If we would like to know what is expected of Christians in terms of the way we are to live in community with one another and in the world in general, we can do no better than follow the guidelines presented by Paul in 12:9–21. In these few verses, Paul summarizes Jewish morality and the teachings of Jesus with twenty-one attributes or characteristics of righteous living. Read the passage and check to see if you also can identify all of these attributes. Which ones are the hardest to live up to? If you were to decide to work harder on one or two of the attributes to enhance your personal and community life, which would you choose?

1 Corinthians

Read 1:1–31 (greeting and report of division); 7:1–16 (instructions regarding marriage); 11:17–34 (instructions regarding the Lord's Supper); 12:1–39 (varieties of gifts and one body); 13:1–13 (the greatest gift is love); and 15:1–58 (the resurrection of Jesus and life after death).

The city of Corinth was in a very strategic location on a small isthmus of land between the Aegean and Adriatic Seas. It was a cosmopolitan city and a center of commerce because of all the trade that came through its port. People of many different national origins lived in Corinth: Greeks, Romans, Syrians, Egyptians, and Jews. In a prominent place in the city was a temple of Aphrodite, the goddess of love, with many temple prostitutes and other accoutrements associated with such pagan worship. What a contrast this would have been to the description of "agape" love Paul presents in 1 Corinthians 13. Whether an intentional strategy of Paul or a providential act of God, it is clear that establishing a Christian church in Corinth would have an impact far beyond its city limits.

Paul first visited Corinth on his second journey and stayed there for eighteen months (Acts 18:1–11). As was his custom, he began by speaking in the synagogue about the good news of Jesus as the Messiah, and he encountered much opposition. He and those who believed his message met in the house of Titius Justus, who lived next door to the synagogue. Crispus, an official of the synagogue, became a believer and was baptized with his whole family. Paul mentions Crispus in the introduction of his letter (1:14).

Paul was the founder of the church in Corinth, and it held a very dear place in his heart because of all the friendship and support that he experienced in that community. Others, including Apollos (see Acts 18:24–28), provided leadership to the church. The roles of Paul and Apollos in the Corinthian church became an issue that Paul addressed in his letter (1:11–17). He declared that the church was not Paul's church, nor was it Apollos's church; rather it was Christ's church and it should not be divided. Aquila and Priscilla, who had left Italy and settled in Corinth, were important members of the church. Paul stayed with them while he was in Corinth because they were also tentmakers (Acts 18:1–4).

After leaving Corinth, Paul spent time in Ephesus, where he received reports about conflicts and wrong thinking in his beloved church in Corinth (1:11; 5:1; 7:1; and 11:18). This first letter to the Corinthians is Paul's effort to address those issues, which included loyalty to various parties rather than loyalty to Jesus Christ (1:ff), sexual immorality among some of the members (5:1–13), marital relations (7:1–40), the eating of food sacrificed to idols (8:1–13), proper celebration of the Lord's Supper (11:17–34), the matter of spiritual gifts and which are of highest importance (chaps. 12–14), and questions about Jesus' resurrection and the nature of life after death (15:1–58).

Galatians

Read all six chapters of Galatians.

Paul's letter "to the churches in Galatia" is addressed to a group of churches rather than one church or individual. Galatia was a province of Rome stretching north and south between the Mediterranean and Black seas in Asia Minor, in what is now modern-day Turkey. Paul visited cities in the southern region of Galatia on his first journey—Derbe, Lystra, and Iconium—and revisited them on subsequent journeys. As with Corinth, Paul had special feelings for the churches in Galatia because it was his preaching of the good news of Jesus Christ that prompted the conversion of many to believe in Jesus as their Lord and Messiah.

The letter begins, as do all of Paul's letters, with a greeting where he identifies himself as an apostle who was commissioned not by human authority but directly through Jesus Christ, who revealed the truth of his resurrection directly to Paul. Included in the greeting is a blessing. Unlike all of his other letters, however, there is no prayer of thanksgiving on behalf of the people of the churches. Instead, Paul moves directly to the two main points of the letter: a defense of himself as a true apostle of Jesus Christ and a denouncement of the false teachings of others who are leading them astray, which he describes as "another gospel" (1:7) and "a gospel contrary to what we proclaimed" (1:8).

In the passage 1:13–2:21 we read the most complete account in the New Testament of Paul's life and work. He describes how he "advanced in Judaism beyond many among my people of the same age, for I was far more zealous for the traditions of my ancestors" (1:14). It is helpful to read this biographical material alongside Paul's words in Acts 22:6–21, where he tells about his life and conversion during his defense before the authorities in Rome. Paul goes into all this detail about his life and conversion in an attempt to authenticate himself and his message as coming directly from God. He writes, "God, who had set me apart before I was born and called me through his grace, was pleased to reveal his Son to me, so that I might proclaim him among the Gentiles" (Gal. 1:15–16).

The false teachers are not identified. Those who have studied Galatians suggest that the ones who have "bewitched" the Christians in Galatia are most likely Jewish Christians who are convinced that it is necessary to keep the demands of the Mosaic law in order to be in right relationship with God, especially the requirement that all male believers be circumcised. He asks the readers, "Did you receive the Spirit by doing the works of the law or by believing what you heard? . . . Well then, does God supply you with the Spirit and work miracles among you by your doing the works of the law, or by your believing what you heard?" (3:2, 5). Paul asks the question and then proceeds in chapters 3 to 5 to develop the argument from Scripture and from experience that their devotion to the law is foolish. He uses as an example the faith of Abraham, who was faithful to God before the law was given. Because of Abraham's faithfulness, God promised that "Abraham shall become a great and mighty nation, and all the nations of the earth shall be blessed in him" (Gen. 18:18).

The essence of Paul's message can be summed up in the words of two passages: "We know that a person is justified not by the works of the law but through faith in Jesus Christ. And we have come to believe in Christ Jesus, so that we might be justified by faith in Christ, and not by doing the works of the law, because no one will be justified by the works of the law" (2:16). And, "There is no longer Jew or Greek . . . slave or free . . . male or female; for all of you are one in Christ Jesus. And if you belong to Christ, then you are Abraham's offspring, heirs according to the promise" (3:28–29).

Philippians

Read all four chapters of Philippians.

Paul's letter to the Christians in Philippi is quite different than the three letters we reviewed above. In his letter to Rome, Paul presents a carefully thought-out theological understanding of the Christian faith. Paul deals with a number of internal issues in his first letter to the church in Corinth. The letter to the Galatians is angry and stern; Paul asserts his credibility as an apostle and criticizes the church for accepting the false teachings of those who require obedience to the law of Moses in order to be a believer in Jesus Christ. Paul's letter to the church in Philippi, on the other hand, is a warm, friendly, encouraging letter written by someone who cares very much about those to whom he is writing and who appreciates their support of him.

Philippi was a prominent and prosperous Roman colony in the days of the early church. Rome was noted for building major roads to connect the far reaches of the empire with its various constituencies. One of those roads, known as the Egnatian Way, went through Philippi, connecting Byzantium to the east with the seaports on the Adriatic to the west, which would provide easy access, across the sea, to Rome. Philippi was the first city Paul visited in Macedonia after having a dream of a man calling him to come to them. As was the custom in Roman cities, women played prominent roles in the civil and commercial life of the community. This was also true of the church in Philippi where Lydia, a dealer in purple cloth and a worshiper of God, became the first convert (Acts 16:14–15).

The letter begins as most of his other letters with a greeting and then a prayer of thanksgiving for "your sharing in the gospel from the first day until now" (Phil. 1:5). This is a very warm and affirming epistle in which Paul expresses his love and appreciation for the Christians in Philippi. He tells them, "I thank my God every time I remember you" (1:3). He addresses them as "beloved" twice (1:12 and 2:12). He expresses how much he desires to visit them again when he is able (1:8 and 4:1), and in his closing words Paul thanks the church for the support and gifts they offered to him.

Paul is in prison (1:14, 17, and 19), though it is not clear from which city or prison he wrote the letter. The consensus is that he did not write the letter from prison in Rome but wrote it from an unnamed prison relatively close to Philippi, sometime about 55 CE. He also wrote Ephesians, Colossians, and Philemon from prison.

In addition to expressing his appreciation, Paul writes to affirm and encourage the Christians in Philippi. His words of guidance include, "Only, live your life in a manner worthy of the gospel of Christ" (1:27); "Work out your own salvation with fear and trembling; for it is God who is at work in you, enabling you both to will and to work for his good pleasure" (2:12–13); and "Brothers and sisters, join in imitating me" (3:17) and "stand firm in the Lord in this way, my beloved" (4:1).

There is one major concern Paul has regarding his friends. In Philippi, like in Corinth and Galatia, there are false teachers, whom Paul calls "dogs" and "evil workers" who "mutilate the flesh" (3:2), who would have them believe that they must be circumcised according to the law of Moses, in order to be fully accepted into the household of faith. He counters this false teaching with testimony from his own experience as "a Hebrew born of Hebrews," a Pharisee, and "as to righteousness under the law, blameless" (3:5–6). He challenges his readers to believe that righteousness "comes through faith in Christ, the righteousness from God based on faith" (3:9). His words are more of affirmation and guidance than scolding as to the Galatians.

1 and 2 Thessalonians

Read all eight short chapters of 1 and 2 Thessalonians.

The city of Thessalonica is approximately eighty miles west of Philippi on the major trade route, Via Egnatia, between Byzantium in the east near the Black Sea and the seaports to the west on the Adriatic Sea. It was a free city governed by a Greek legal system rather than Roman. It was a cosmopolitan city with worshipers of many religions, all with their temples and idols in the vicinity. There was also a very strong Jewish community.

The two letters to the church in Thessalonica appear to be quite similar. However, many Bible interpreters doubt that the same author wrote them both. While there is universal agreement that Paul wrote the first letter, many questions exist about the author of the second. The critical passage in 2 Thessalonians is 2:2: "by word or by letter, as though from us, to the effect that the day of the Lord is already here." This would be a clear contradiction of the thrust of 1 Thessalonians where the "day of the Lord" is an event expected in the future. Also, the emphatic statement in 3:17 of the second letter regarding Paul writing it in his own hand seems to many to be overstated and unlike Paul's other letters where he indicated he had written the letter or the conclusion in his own hand.

1 Thessalonians is believed to have been the first letter of Paul in the New Testament written sometime around 50 CE. Paul wrote the letter from Corinth not long after he, Timothy, and Sivanus (or Silas as in Acts 17:1) escaped from

Thessalonica due to the threats on their lives from the Jews and "some ruffians" (Acts 17:5). As a result of their preaching in the synagogue in Thessalonica, "Some of them were persuaded [to believe that Jesus was the promised Messiah] and joined Paul and Silas, as did a great many of the devout Greeks and not a few of the leading women" (Acts 17:4). These are the converts to whom Paul addresses the first letter.

Paul had great affection for the young church in Thessalonica and he was very proud of them: "And you became imitators of us and of the Lord, for in spite of persecution you received the word with joy inspired by the Holy Spirit, so that you became an example to all the believers in Macedonia and in Achaia" (1 Thess. 1:6–7). Paul was aware of the persecution they were suffering from the Jews, and he yearned to know how they were doing. So he sent Timothy to check on them, and after Timothy returned with an encouraging report that they were remaining steadfast in their faith in Jesus Christ, Paul was greatly encouraged.

In the first part of chapter 4, Paul urged the Christians in Thessalonica to live in harmony with God's will for them and with love and respect for one another. From 4:13 through 5:11 Paul instructs them regarding Jesus' return, the end times, and what happens to those who have died before the Lord's return. It appears that Paul, at this time, expects the return of Jesus will come in his lifetime. That view is not seen in his later letters. He assures the believers that their loved ones who have died in Christ will be the first to rise. "Then we who are alive, who are left, will be caught up on the clouds together with them to meet the Lord in the air, and so we will be with the Lord forever" (4:17). Paul admonishes his readers to encourage one another in this assurance and to continue to be faithful in their devotion to Jesus Christ. This view of anticipating the "day of Lord" as an event in the future is in stark contrast with the view in the second letter that states "the day of the Lord is already here" (2 Thess. 2:2).

Chapter Eight
The Revelation to John

The last book of the Bible, and the New Testament, is The Revelation to John, which is usually just called "Revelation." Many people call the book "Revelations," which is incorrect, even though there are a number of revelations in the book. The title is derived from the opening words of chapter 1, "The revelation of Jesus Christ . . . to his servant John."

Revelation is the only complete book in the Bible that is an example of apocalyptic literature. Daniel 7–12 in the Old Testament and Mark 13 are other examples of apocalyptic writings. The Greek word *apokalypsis* means to "unveil," "uncover," or "reveal" and is translated in the New Testament as *revelation*.

Apocalyptic writings usually have the following characteristics: a secret revelation is given to a seer or prophet, the revelation is imparted in a dream or vision, the revelation is mediated by an angel, and the revelation is not self-explanatory but is encoded with signs and symbols. The Revelation to John fulfills all of these characteristics.

Prayer Prompted by Scripture

Revelation contains many hymns and prayers addressed to God. Our prayer in this chapter is prompted by several of these hymns and prayers. Read the passages as your prayer. When you have read them all, go back and select one of the hymns or prayers and copy it to a blank sheet of paper. After you have copied the words from Revelation, continue by writing several more lines that will then be your prayer. Let the words of Revelation prompt thoughts, feelings, thanksgiving, beliefs, or concerns in your mind so that you will write words for your own prayer or hymn to God.

Holy, holy, holy, the Lord God the Almighty,
who was and is and is to come. (4:8b)
You are worthy, our Lord and God, to receive glory and honor and power,
for you created all things, and by your will they existed and were created. (4:11)
To the one seated on the throne and to the Lamb
be blessing and honor and glory and might forever and ever! (5:13b)
The kingdom of the world has become the kingdom of our Lord
and of his Messiah, and he will reign forever and ever. (11:15b)
Great and amazing are your deeds, Lord God the Almighty!
Just and true are your ways, King of the nations!
Lord, who will not fear and glorify your name? For you alone are holy.
All nations will come and worship before you,
for your judgments have been revealed. (15:3–4)
Praise our God, all you his servants,
And all who fear him, small and great. (19:5)
Hallelujah! For the Lord our God the Almighty reigns.
Let us rejoice and exult and give him the glory. (19:6b–7)

Select a verse or two or perhaps just one line. Transcribe those words to a sheet of paper and then continue writing whatever words come to your mind to express your thoughts, beliefs, praises, thanksgiving, or concerns as your prayer to God.

Background for Understanding Revelation

Tradition has held that the apostle John was the author of the Gospel and the three epistles that bear his name, and the book of Revelation. However, most biblical scholars agree that the apostle John is not the author of Revelation. Several passages within the book support this view. First, the author speaks of himself as a servant of God (1:1). Second, he indicates that he shares the same persecutions as his readers and that he has been exiled to the island of Patmos from which he writes (1:9). Third, the author speaks of the twelve apostles as being the "twelve foundations" on which the new Jerusalem will be built (21:14). And those who are experts in the language, theology, and style of biblical writings conclude that Revelation has very little similarity with the other four books of the New Testament that are attributed John. We also learn that the author serves as a prophet when he refers to his writing as a prophetic book. He mentions this once in the first chapter (1:3) and four times in the last chapter (22:7, 10, 18, 19) with the statement "words of the prophecy" or "the prophecy of this book." We discover that the author is very familiar with seven particular churches in Asia Minor to whom he addresses the book, or letter. He could have been a preacher or prophet who traveled among those churches. And it is clear that the writer is very knowledgeable about the Hebrew Scriptures. He uses many images, events, and quotations from the Hebrew Scriptures with which his readers would also have been familiar. This becomes part of the "code" that the readers would have understood but that would have been nonsense to any Roman officials who might have read the book.

Revelation was written in a time when believers in Jesus Christ were being persecuted for their faith. It is difficult to determine exactly when Revelation was written, though there seems to be a consensus that it was written in the late first century when Domitian reigned as emperor from 81–96 CE. During his reign, Christians were persecuted throughout the empire. On several occasions, as he recounts a vision, the writer indicates that the faithful are about to suffer or have suffered for their faith. One example is 6:9–11: "When he opened the fifth seal, I saw under the altar the souls of those who had been slaughtered for the word of God and for the testimony they had given. . . . They were each given a white robe and told to rest a little longer, until the number would be complete both of their fellow servants and of their brothers and sisters, who were soon to be killed as they themselves had been killed." This letter, first to the Christians of the seven churches and second to all believers who might read the book, is intended to give encouragement and hope in a time of persecution. The writer desired to help them stay steadfast in their faith and commitment to Jesus Christ in the midst of the very severe trials they were facing.

An Overview of Revelation

Revelation is a complex and mysterious book that confuses most readers when they attempt to read and understand it without responsible guidance. The book has also been the subject of many interpretations and misinterpretations. Those who read the book as a prediction of what is happening in our world today, or what will happen in the future, more often than not are misinterpreting the book. The author wrote to a specific constituency of believers in a particular historical setting in order to encourage them to remain faithful in a time of great persecution by the Roman authorities. To begin to understand the book of Revelation we must try to understand the world of the writer and the readers, and attempt to decipher the "code" in which it is written. Those who read the book in this way are likely to interpret the book more responsibly. Because it is such a complex book, we will be able to review only a few of its main features and highlight some of its contents. I commend two other excellent resources for a more comprehensive, in-depth study of Revelation.[1] Let's look at a few of the sections and a couple of features of Revelation.

Prologue (1:1–3)

The three verses of the prologue provide a lot of clues for what is to come. We have already commented on several points in these three verses. The revelation is of Jesus Christ. It is a revelation of what "must soon take place," in the first century, not the next or the twenty-first century. The revelation is made known by an angel to "his servant John." Verse three begins with "blessed," which is the first of seven beatitudes in Revelation (14:13; 16:15; 19:9; 20:6; 22:7, 14). Those who read aloud the words of the prophecy will be blessed as will those who hear the words.

Act 1: The seven churches (1:4–3:22)

John addresses the letter to seven churches in Asia Minor. He writes, "I was in the spirit on the Lord's day" (1:10). He experienced a vision of the Son of Man, who instructs him to "write what you have seen, what is, and what is to take place after this" (1:19). There are images of seven lampstands and seven stars, which he explains in 1:20 as representing the seven churches: Ephesus, Smyrna, Pergamum, Thyatira, Sardis, Philadelphia, and Laodicea. If you look at a map with the seven cities in Asia Minor identified, you will see that beginning with Ephesus the churches are in sequence along a route that goes north, turns east, and then goes south, ending up at Laodicea. The words to each church follow a similar pattern with five parts.

1. First, there is an *introductory statement* that identifies the authority of the one who is speaking. "These are the words of him who holds the seven stars in his right hand, who walks among the seven golden lampstands" (2:1). To each of the

1. James A. Walther Sr., *The Book of Revelation: Visions for a Church in Crisis* (Pittsburgh: The Kerygma Program, 1989), and Bruce M. Metzger, *Breaking the Code: Understanding the Book of Revelation* (Nashville: Abingdon Press, 1993). Each resource has both a participant's book and a leader's guide.

other six churches there is a similar, but different, image that identifies Christ as the one who speaks. Other images include "the first and the last, who was dead and came to life" (2:8), "him who has the sharp two-edged sword" (2:12), and "the Son of God, who has eyes like a flame of fire" (2:18).

2. Each church is next addressed with the words, "I know." This phrase introduces *words of commendation* for the church's faithfulness and perseverance; for instance, "I know your works—your love, faith, service, and patient endurance" (2:19). The words to the churches in Sardis and Laodicea are not as affirming.

3. Words of commendation are followed by *words of judgment* that are introduced by the phrase, "But I have this against you . . ." This is the case with four of the seven churches. For instance, the words of judgment against the church in Ephesus are, "You have abandoned the love you had at first" (2:4).

4. The fourth section addressed to each church is *words of admonition.* These words are introduced by "remember," "beware," "repent," "hold fast," or "be earnest." These words of admonition challenge the believers to remain faithful in the difficult times they face. An example is to the church in Sardis: "Remember then what you received and heard; obey it, and repent" (3:3).

5. The address to each church concludes with words of hope and promise that are introduced by a phrase, "He who conquers . . ." Those who overcome the threats to their faith will receive blessings from God. There are words of hope and promise for each church, even for the Christians of Laodicea who were told earlier that their works "are neither cold nor hot" (3:15). This church also receives a promise of "I will give a place with me on my throne, just as I myself conquered and sat down with my Father on his throne" (3:21).

Act 2: Visions and the seven seals (4:1–8:6)

When I was in seminary in the late 1950s my New Testament professor was John Wick Bowman, who wrote a book, *The Drama of the Book of Revelation*,[2] which

2. John Wick Bowman, *The First Christian Drama—The Book of Revelation* (Philadelphia: Westminster Press, 1968); originally, *The Drama of the Book of Revelation* (Philadelphia: Westminster Press, 1955).

was my first introduction to Revelation. A unique feature of his interpretation is viewing Revelation as a drama with a prologue, eight acts, and an epilogue. He presents the letters to seven churches as Act 1, followed by the visions and seven seals as Act 2. We will spend some time with this act as representative of the six acts that follow.

In one sense it is helpful to read Act 2 as if you were the stage manager for the drama. The curtains part and John sees a door open to heaven. There on the stage is a "throne with one seated on the throne! . . . Around the throne are twenty-four thrones, and seated on the thrones are twenty-four elders, dressed in white robes, with golden crowns on their heads" (4:2–4). There are flashes of lightning, peals of thunder, seven flaming torches, and in the foreground is a sea of glass like crystal. Added to the scene are four living creatures, each with six wings. The four creatures sing day and night, "Holy, holy, holy, the Lord God the Almighty, who was and is and is to come" (4:8). The twenty-four elders "fall before the one seated on the throne . . . cast their crowns before the throne, singing, 'You are worthy, our Lord and our God, to receive glory and honor and power" (4:11). The stage setting continues to build: "in the right hand of the one seated on the throne a scroll . . . sealed with seven seals" (5:1). "Between the throne and the four living creatures and among the elders a Lamb standing as if it had been slaughtered" (5:6). The Lamb takes the scroll from the one on the throne, and the four creatures and elders fall before the Lamb and sing a new song of praise to the Lamb. Then the Lamb opens each of the seven seals.

The opening of the first four seals is accompanied by a voice saying "Come!" and out come four horses each of a different color, followed by "the souls of those who had been slaughtered for the word of God" (6:9) at the opening of the fifth seal. The opening of the sixth seal is connected to an earthquake, angels standing at the four corners of the earth, and a fifth angel "having the seal of the living God . . . saying, 'Do not damage the earth . . . until we have marked the servants of our God with a seal on their foreheads' . . . and the number of those who were sealed, one hundred forty-four thousand" (7:2–4). "When the Lamb opened the seventh seal, there was silence in heaven for about half an hour. And I saw the seven angels who stand before God, and seven trumpets were given to them" (8:1–2). This concludes Act 2. In Act 3 the seven angels with their seven trumpets sound out seven woes upon the earth.

When we read this portion of Revelation (4:1–8:6) it is impossible to make sense of the text unless we use our imaginations and try to discern the meaning of the many symbols that are "on stage" in this part of the drama. We have already mentioned that the book is written with many symbols, images, and references to the Hebrew Scriptures as well as to the message of the gospel of Jesus Christ. If we can discern the meaning of these "code words," then perhaps we can come to some understanding of what John was trying to communicate. Interpreters are not of one mind as to the meanings of these symbols, but as I read their suggestions it seems to me that we come close to understanding them when we make the connections as outlined in the chart on page 84.

It would be helpful to reread Revelation 4:1–8:6 with this chart in front of you. As you read these chapters, imagine yourself present with the Christians of the seven churches who are experiencing persecution and the threat of death if they were to testify to their faith in Jesus as the Lord and Messiah. If you were one of the believers of the late first century, all of the images would be familiar to you. You would recognize the many allusions to passages in the Hebrew Scriptures. This message from John would help you put into perspective what you know of God and God's will in relation to the persecution you experience. John's words would be read and heard as a message of hope. You would be reassured that God is Lord of all the earth and all history and God's Word is the final authority. Though you will experience hardship, persecution, and perhaps even death, you should not fear because in the final day God will lift you up to victory and new life.

The drama of Revelation continues (8:7–19:10)

In this chapter it is not possible to go into the same amount of detail about chapters 8 through 22 as we did with chapters 1 through 7 in the previous two sections. We will summarize the contents of these fifteen chapters, Act 3 through Act 8 and the epilogue, using Dr. Bowman's way of viewing Revelation.

- Act 3 (8:7–11:19) describes the sounding of seven trumpets pronouncing judgments upon the earth, and with each trumpet there is a corresponding calamity similar to seven of the plagues visited upon the Egyptians at the time of the exodus of the Israelites from Egypt.
- Act 4 (12:1–13:18 presents seven visions of the dragon's kingdom. This section symbolizes the battle between the forces of good and evil presented as a cosmic struggle between a woman, her son, and the archangel Michael (representing the Messiah) and the great dragon and the beasts (representing Satan and the forces opposed to God's reign). Another code number, six hundred sixty-six, is used to represent the value of a person's name in Hebrew, possibly Nero Caesar, who persecuted the Christians in Rome in vicious ways.
- Act 5 (14:1–20) includes seven visions of worshipers of the Lamb. The number one hundred and forty-four thousand appears again, this time in reference to the martyrs

This image . . .	symbolizes . . .
Throne	God's sovereignty
One seated on the throne	God
Rainbow	God's covenant
Twenty-four elders	Twelve patriarchs of Israel and twelve apostles of the new Israel
Flashes of lightning and peals of thunder	God's appearance at Sinai
Seven spirits	Seven archangels before God
Four creatures	Matthew, Mark, Luke, John
The number seven	Perfection, completion
Scroll	God's final word or plan
Seven seals	Scroll is completely sealed
Lion of the tribe of Judah, the root of David	King of Israel, the Messiah
The Lamb slaughtered	Jesus crucified
Seven horns, eyes, spirits	Power and presence of God
Myriad of myriads	Innumerable angelic beings
White horse and rider	Warfare
Bright red horse and rider	Death in battle
Black horse and rider	Famine
Pale green horse and rider	Death and Hades
Black sun, red moon, and stars falling	Anticipation of the Day of the Lord
One hundred forty-four thousand	12 x 12 x 1,000 is the highest possible number; represents all the people of God
Seven trumpets	Sign of the end of time
Incense	Prayers of the saints

who remained faithful. There are visions of the Lamb standing on Mount Zion, four angels, a voice from heaven, and the Son of Man sitting on a white cloud. These visions give hope and promise to those who remain faithful and warn of the wrath of God upon those who oppose God.

- Act 6 (15:1–16:21) tells of seven visions of angels with bowls of God's wrath. As with the vision of the seven trumpets and the related woes, so in this series of seven visions of bowls of wrath, the plagues of Exodus are recalled. The dominant theme in the previous section was a message of encouragement, but in this section the dominant theme is the wrath of God directed toward the "beast," which for John represents Rome and the emperor. In the end the beast will be destroyed and God's reign will prevail.
- Act 7 (17:1–19:10) portrays seven visions of the fall of Babylon. Throughout Revelation, Babylon is the symbol John uses to represent Rome. In addition, Rome is likened to a "great whore." The passage that sums it up is, "The woman was clothed in purple and scarlet, and adorned with gold and jewels and pearls . . . and on her forehead was written a name, a mystery: 'Babylon the great, mother of whores and of earth's abominations.' And I saw that the woman was drunk with the blood of the saints and the blood of the witnesses to Jesus" (17:4–6). In the end the beast, Babylon, and the whore are defeated and "the twenty-four elders and the four living creatures fell down and worshiped God who is seated on the throne, saying, 'Amen. Hallelujah!'" (19:4).
- Act 8 (19:11–21:8) is the closing act in which there are seven visions describing the end of Satan's reign and the beginning of God's reign. In this section is the only mention of a thousand-year period when Satan would be bound and those who had been killed because they would not "worship the beast or its image" would come back to life and reign with Jesus. There has been much debate about the nature of these thousand years, with many books championing one view or another. This is

not the place to enter the debate, but to point to the one passage in the Bible on which the various doctrines of millennialism are based. The scene closes with a vision of the holy city, the new Jerusalem coming down from heaven. The one on the throne, God, speaks for the first time in Revelation: "'See, the home of God is among mortals. He will dwell with them; they will be his peoples, and God himself will be with them; he will wipe away every tear from their eyes. Death will be no more; mourning and crying and pain will be no more, for the first things have passed away.' And the one who was seated on the throne said, 'See, I am making all things new.' . . . Then he said to me, 'It is done. I am the Alpha and the Omega, the beginning and the end' " (21:3–5).

- The epilogue (21:9–22:21) of the drama of Revelation uses many images to symbolize the new Jerusalem. The details describing the city are elaborate, and the dimensions of its boundaries are immense. In the new Jerusalem there is no temple because the Lord God Almighty and the Lamb (Jesus) are the temple in the midst of the city (21:22). The writer concludes with two blessings—"Blessed is the one who keeps the words of the prophecy of this book" (22:7) and "Blessed are those who wash their robes, so that they will have the right to the tree of life and may enter the city by the gates" (22:14)—and a benediction: "Amen. Come, Lord Jesus! The grace of the Lord Jesus be with all the saints. Amen" (22:20–21). Revelation 22:17 is an evangelical invitation placing the whole message in the setting of the church.

Part 2

LEADER'S GUIDE

Guidelines for Bible Study Leaders

The Course's Origin

This course was first presented as part of the adult education program of the First Presbyterian Church in Livermore, California, in 1986. At the time, I was a parish associate for the church. Pat Griggs was chair of the Adult Education and Nurture Committee. She said to me one day, "We need a Bible study course for those folks who think everyone else in the church knows more about the Bible than they do. We need a course that will provide a helpful overview of the whole Bible and will introduce the class members to basic tools and skills for Bible study, and at the same time be fun and interesting. We want you to teach that course." Well, one doesn't decline an invitation like that, especially when the chair of the committee is one's wife. The original course was for fourteen sessions and covered the whole Bible. The course in this book features only the New Testament. A second volume, *The Bible from Scratch: The Old Testament for Beginners*, is also available from Westminster John Knox Press.

If you have already led a group through the course on the Old Testament, then what follows might be redundant and you may want to just skim or perhaps skip this material. If you are new to these two resources, then I am sure you will find this introduction very helpful as you get started in your planning to teach *The Bible from Scratch: The New Testament for Beginners*.

Goals of the Course

As I planned this course, I had several goals in mind for the group members. I expected that the participants would do the following:

- Become comfortable using the Bible by being able to find books, chapters, and verses more easily.
- Gain a sense of the general "sweep" of the biblical story: to identify familiar persons and events, to see their connection to one another, and to get a sense of chronology.
- Be introduced to basic Bible study tools such as the concordance, Bible dictionary, atlas, and commentary.
- Appreciate the value of having a variety of translations, to recognize the differences between them, and to read at least one translation in addition to their favorite.
- Enjoy studying the Bible with others.
- Develop the habit of reading the Bible regularly.

These goals were achieved by many of the participants, especially those who were present for all the sessions. Hardly a week went by without one or more of the participants expressing delight in what they had discovered that week. About ten of the twenty-five class members did commit to further intensive study in courses guided by the Kerygma Program Bible study resources. One of the members informed me several years later that he was teaching a senior high Bible study class in his new church and was using his notes from this course as a basis for his planning and teaching.

Basic Teaching Principles

As I prepared the course, I was very intentional about implementing a number of basic principles for effective teaching and leading. The foundational principle was to attempt to involve everyone in every part of every session every week.

That's a big goal! It was not possible to succeed with everyone every week, but there were many opportunities for individuals to participate every week, and most did. You will see this principle present in all of the session plans that follow. I had at least a dozen other principles in mind as I designed the course:

- The leader serves best as companion and guide in the journey of the course.
- The leader provides sufficient information, but not so much that the joy of discovery by the participants is lost.
- Motivation for learning involves enjoying and completing tasks and making choices.
- It is often better to use selected portions of a resource rather than the complete resource.
- Participants learn best when a variety of activities and resources are used in order to respond to their different interests, needs, and learning styles.
- Participants need to be invited to express their feelings, ideas, and beliefs in creative ways that are appropriate to them and to the subject matter.
- Everyone needs opportunities to share what they understand and believe.
- Open-ended questions invite interpretation, reflection, and application.
- Persons are nurtured in faith when they share their faith stories with one another.
- All teaching and learning happens in planned and unplanned ways and is for the purpose of increasing biblical literacy and faithful discipleship.
- The Bible becomes the living Word of God when teachers and learners see their own faith stories expressed in Scripture.
- The Bible provides many resources to prompt our praying, our confessing of faith, and our commitment to ministry.

Room Arrangement

Arrange the room where you meet in such a way that participants are seated at tables. Tables are very important in that they provide space for all of the materials—and the coffee cups. Tables also suggest that we are going to work; we are not here to just sit and listen to a lecture.

Unless everyone knows everyone else in the group, members need name tags. Set up a table with hot water and makings for coffee, tea, and hot chocolate just inside the entrance to the room so everyone can get a cup and then find a seat. If you have a small group, arrange the tables in a rectangle or square so that everyone can see all the other members of the group. With a small group, you will be able to be seated with them. On the other hand, if you have a large group, arrange the tables in a fan shape pointed toward the front so the participants can see the leader standing at the front of the group with a white board, newsprint easel, or screen for the overhead projector.

Resources

During the first week, be sure to provide Bibles for those who do not bring one. Continue to provide Bibles for those occasions when it is important for everyone to have the same translation and edition so that you can all look at the same pages at the same time. However, continue to encourage everyone to bring his or her own Bible. In addition to the Bibles, borrow from the church library, the pastor's library, and your own library as many copies of concise concordances, Bible dictionaries, and Bible atlases as you can find. It is important to put these resources in the hands of the group members so they can practice using the tools for Bible study. You will be surprised to see how many persons buy new study Bibles, dictionaries, and other resources after they are exposed to them during the course.

A church library will not ordinarily have enough Bible dictionaries for each person to have one with which to work. For those sessions where members are responsible for searching for information about a book, person, or event in the Bible, make photocopies of the appropriate articles in a Bible dictionary, encyclopedia, or atlas. For onetime use, for one class, this is not a violation of the copyright laws.

Be sure to provide paper and pencils for those who don't bring them. Almost all of the activity sheets to be used by the participants are at the end of the respective session plans for which they will be used. The session plans inlude several other activity sheets that you will need to reproduce for the participants.

Time

I planned each session to be an hour in length. If you have less than an hour, you will have to make some adjustments. It will be better to leave out an activity than to rush class members through all of the planned activities. Perhaps it would be possible in your situation to schedule more than eight sessions. There is probably enough material here for ten to twelve sessions. If you have that much time, you will truly be able to deal with everything carefully, without hurrying.

If you and your group have already studied the companion to this Bible study, *The Bible from Scratch: The Old Testament for Beginners*, you may decide to skip session 1 in this course, which is mostly a repeat of session 1 in the other course. On the other hand, if you have members of the group who were not involved in the Old Testament course or who would like a little refresher on some of the basic skills, then it would be a good idea to begin with session 1.

A Final Word

As you prepare to teach this course, it is essential that you read each chapter of part 1 as you consider your teaching strategy for each session of the course. You should assume that many, though not all, of the participants will have read the respective chapter before coming to the class session, and you should be as familiar with the material as they are. Exploring the Bible with fellow pilgrims on the journey of faith will be for them and for you a challenging, inspiring, growing, and satisfying experience. May God bless you with many discoveries and much joy on this journey. If you and the members of your Bible study group have found this course to be helpful, you may want to plan for a second course on the Old Testament based on *The Bible from Scratch: The Old Testament for Beginners.*

Session One

Introducing the New Testament

BEFORE THE SESSION

Focus of the Session

In this first session, it will be important to take time for participants to become comfortable with the room, with one another, and with you as the leader. It will also be a time for getting acquainted with some of the basics of reading and studying the Bible, such as using the table of contents, practicing how to locate passages, reviewing punctuation of Bible passage citations, identifying Bible books by their abbreviations, practicing with a concordance, and sharing results of the Bible Skills and Tools Inventory. In addition, there will be an opening Prayer Prompted by Scripture activity featuring the Beatitudes. This session includes a lot of activities, which means that you will have to decide which one(s) to omit if you do not have enough time. Or you could decide to spend two weeks on this session.

Advanced Preparation

- Read all of the passages suggested in the material for the participants.
- Read the introductory articles in a study Bible.
- Read articles in a Bible dictionary that deal with *Scripture, translation, gospel, epistle,* and *language.*
- Bring to class at least one copy each of a concordance in a study Bible, a concise concordance, and a comprehensive, or complete, concordance.
- Gather as many concise concordances as you are able. If you don't have enough so that each pair of persons can share a copy, then it will be important to copy excerpts from a concise concordance. You will find additional directions in the session plan.

Physical Arrangements

Reread the section of the introduction that offers suggestions regarding room arrangement, resources and materials, and refreshments. You should have everything ready and in order for the first session. First impressions are very important, especially for those who are new to Bible study.

DURING THE SESSION

Welcome of Participants

Arrive at class early enough to set up the refreshments and to have everything ready before the first person arrives. Ask the participants to sign in and make name tags for themselves. Greet each one by name and with a warm welcome. If you have a display of books and resources, invite participants to spend time browsing before the session begins. As the group gathers, be sure to remind them of the four suggestions on pages 5–6. Check to see who needs to borrow a Bible and give them one. Also, encourage them to bring a Bible next week.

Opening Prayer

On pages 4–5 is the litany prayer based on the Beatitudes from Matthew 5:1–12. You or another member of the group will read each statement from the Beatitudes, and the group will read/pray the response. Before beginning, call everyone's attention to the last statement and point out that there is no printed response. Tell the group that there will be a half-minute of silence after that statement is read; during that silence, everyone should write or think of a brief prayer response. Then, you will read the beatitude again and invite members to share their brief prayers. There are two questions following the prayer on page 5. Spend just a few minutes discussing those questions.

Getting Acquainted

Invite the participants to introduce themselves by sharing their names and an early memory associated with the Bible. Some will have memories from childhood, while others may have memories of more recent experiences. This is not a time for long stories, just brief vignettes. If you have a large group, you may want to form smaller groups for this exercise. Remind the participants that they can get up to refill their beverage cup at any time and that you are open to any questions they may have at any time.

Bible Basics

Ask everyone to turn in their Bibles to the table of contents and the introductory pages that follow. People will have different translations. Affirm whatever translation they are using and that the group will be able to learn more because of the variety that is available. You could do several things with the group. Depending on the amount of time you have, you may want to select from among the following suggestions:

- Focus on the books of the New Testament. Call attention to the four different kinds of books listed there: gospels, "history," letters or epistles, and Revelation. Notice that some of the letters are addressed to churches, some to individuals, and one to a group (Hebrews).
- Ask participants to share some of the "things I notice" if they completed that activity on page 8.
- Practice pronouncing some of the more difficult names of Bible books.

- Spend a few minutes responding to some of the "questions I have" that they wrote on page 8.
- Spend a few minutes practicing identifying books by their abbreviations by writing them one at a time on the white board or sheet of newsprint. Start with a few that are fairly obvious, and then use examples that may be a little more difficult.

Next, turn to the first page of the book of Matthew. Ask how many have Bibles with introductions to each book. This may be a good time to make a pitch for purchasing a study Bible. Make your own recommendations or direct them to pages 159–160, where several study Bibles are described. There are several brief activities you can do with the first pages of Matthew.

- Invite participants to share "things I notice."
- Review the skill of reading Bible citations by book, chapter, and verses by writing down some examples and asking for confirmation of what is designated. Be sure to use abbreviations to identify the Bible books.
- Ask persons to share from their list on page 9 any of the "questions I have." Don't spend a lot of time on this. If there are a lot of questions, write them down on a sheet of newsprint with a heading "Loose Ends." Keep this list in front of the class week to week, and be sure to respond to all of the questions before the last session of the class.

Practicing with a Bible Concordance

The participants were introduced to the nature of a concordance in chapter 1, but they haven't experienced using one, unless they already have a concordance at home. It is ideal if you are able to secure enough small or concise concordances so that each pair of persons has access to one. If that is not possible, then be sure to have available examples of several types of concordances to show their differences. If you don't have enough concordances for the participants to use, then it will be necessary to duplicate pages of a concise concordance that include the words for the following activities: *law, greatest, commandment, love, soul, heart,* and *mind.*

1. Ask the participants if they have heard of the passage where Jesus is asked, "Which commandment in the law is the

greatest?" (Matt. 22:36). Several participants will surely raise their hands. Ask them, "How did Jesus answer the question?" Spend a minute recalling that his answer is known as the Great Commandment: "You shall love the Lord your God with all your heart, and with all your soul, and with all your mind" (Matt. 22:37). Then ask, "Does anyone know where to find the passage?" If any know, ask them to find it but not to tell anyone else. Ask the others, "Where would you start looking to find the passage?"

2. Instruct the participants to take a few minutes to attempt to find the passage where Jesus is asked the question, "Which commandment in the law is the greatest?" Allow just a minute or two. The participants will be frustrated, which prepares them to be ready to learn about a tool that will help them find passages they are familiar with but don't know how to locate. Remind the participants that they are limited in their ability to find Bible passages by: 1. what they remember, 2. what they find by chance in their skimming, and 3. what they are directed to find by the leader.

3. Inform the group members that there is a special book/resource/tool designed to help them find familiar passages as well as other passages on a particular topic. That book is a concordance. Show and explain the differences and similarities between concise and comprehensive concordances. As you are doing this, have them look at pages 14–15 where they will see brief examples of each. Check to see if anyone has a simple concordance in the back of his or her Bible.

4. Take time to practice with the concordance. Make a list of key words in the passage referred to above: *law, greatest, commandment, love, soul, heart,* and *mind*. Now, using the concordances or the handouts you prepared, have them find the passage. No doubt they will be led by one or more of the key words to Matthew 22:34–40, Mark 12:28–31, or Luke 10:25–28. When they have found all three passages, spend a few minutes calling attention to the similarities and differences of the three passages.

5. Comment that the words of Jesus' answer in Matthew and Luke are not original to him; he is quoting from the books of the law. This provides an opportunity to introduce the

value of cross-reference notes to find the source of quotes in one book of the Bible from another. Check to see if anyone in the group has a Bible with cross-reference notes. Study Bibles are especially helpful in this matter. If not, use the same key words above to find the original passages in Deuteronomy 6:5 and Leviticus 19:18.

6. If any time remains, and you have a sufficient number of concordances, you could practice finding other familiar passages that members of the group remember but have no idea how to locate.

The Scriptures

Turn to the worksheet titled "The Scriptures," found on page 101. The directions are clear on the worksheet, but review them to be sure everyone knows what is expected. Check to see if all of the passages have been selected. If not, ask if any pairs would be willing to work on their second choice among those that have not been selected. Encourage the class members to work in pairs. One direction to emphasize is that after each in the pair has read the passage, they are to begin discussing the three questions immediately instead of writing and then sharing their answers.

After the pairs have spent about ten minutes on the passage, ask participants to leave their partners and team up with another person or two for another few minutes to compare notes regarding their respective passages.

Save the last task of completing the sentence for the end of the session.

Bible Skills and Tools Inventory

If participants received their book a week or so before the class began, they may have completed the Bible Skills and Tools Inventory found on page 12. If that is not the case, you may need to provide about five minutes for them to complete it now. Afterward, ask for a show of hands on each item, and have someone take notes on the numbers and the comments in their responses. This will be useful information for you. As you ask for responses, assure the participants that they should not feel embarrassed or proud of their answers but that it is helpful to know that others have had as much, or as little, experience in studying the Bible as they have. The purpose of the course is to increase members' familiarity with the Bible and their confidence in using the Bible and other Bible study tools.

Closing

Ask the participants to take thirty seconds to complete the sentence that begins, "The Scriptures are . . ." After they have created their sentences, you have the ingredients of a litany. Invite members to share their sentences. After each has shared, the whole group will respond in unison, "O God, help us to learn and love your Holy Word." It would be good to write this unison response on a sheet of newsprint or on a chalkboard so they will know what to say.

The Scriptures

1. Work in pairs. Each pair should work on *one* of the following passages:

Matthew 4:1–11	"But [Jesus] answered, 'It is written . . .''
Luke 4:16–21	Jesus stands up to read the Scriptures.
Luke 24:13–35	Jesus explains to his companions the Scriptures.
Acts 8:26–38	"The passage of the scripture that he was reading . . ."
Acts 17:1–15	"[They] examined the scriptures every day . . ."
Romans 15:1–13	"By the encouragement of the scriptures . . ."
2 Timothy 3:10–17	"All scripture is inspired by God."

2. After reading the passage, reflect on three questions:

   What is the specific Scripture reference or content, if any?

   What seems to be the purpose or use of the Scriptures in this passage?

   What appear to be the results from speaking, hearing, or reading the Scriptures?

Complete the following sentence:

The Scriptures are ____

____

____

____

____

____

____

____

____

Session Two

The Gospel of Matthew

BEFORE THE SESSION

Focus of the Session

It will not be possible to do an in-depth overview of the content of the Gospel of Matthew, but we will be able to focus on several parts of the book. In addition, we will work on two basic skills: 1. identifying the role of footnotes and practicing how to read and use them, and 2. comparing a passage in Matthew with a passage dealing with the same narrative in Luke. You may also want to spend a little time summarizing some of the important characteristics and key passages of Matthew.

Advanced Preparation

- Read the passages suggested in the material for the participants.

- Read one or more introductory articles for Matthew in a study Bible and/or Bible dictionary.
- Read articles in a Bible dictionary that deal with *gospel, synoptic, the Lord's Prayer, the genealogy of Jesus,* and *the Sermon on the Mount.*
- Gather Bibles from the sanctuary or classrooms that are all the same and have footnote references. This will make the practice with footnotes easier.

DURING THE SESSION

Welcome of Participants

There will likely be persons coming to this session who were not at the first session. Be sure they are welcomed and briefed about what to expect. Greet all of the participants and encourage them to browse among the various translations of the Bible you have displayed on a table.

Opening Prayer

The opening prayer is the Lord's Prayer, which was also the focus of the Prayer Prompted by Scripture activity in chapter 2. Some of the participants in your group will have already completed the steps of that activity prior to class. You could choose from several activities to open this session or combine two or more of them.

- If you plan to use all of the activities suggested in this session, you could begin with just praying the Lord's Prayer in unison according to the custom of your church.
- If there are several translations of the Bible scattered among the members of your group, you could invite several persons to read Matthew 6:9–13 from their translations and then conclude with praying in unison.
- You could bring a cassette or a CD of a recording of the Lord's Prayer for the participants to listen to as part of the opening prayer.
- The ecumenical version of the Lord's Prayer is on page 17. You could pray that prayer in unison.

- If you have time during the week, you could gather a collection of photographs from magazines that present in a visual way some of the concepts that are part of the Lord's Prayer. Scatter the photographs on a table or shelf and invite participants to select one photograph that illustrates for them one concept in the prayer. During a reciting of the Lord's Prayer, ask members to lift up their photograph for others to see when the word or phrase of the prayer is spoken. Pray in unison, slowly, with eyes open.
- After the opening prayer, take a few minutes to discuss together the three questions that are on page 17. Don't take too much time for this unless the discussion is proving to be very productive.

Compare Birth Narratives

Call attention to the "genealogy of Jesus the Messiah, the son of David, the son of Abraham" (Matt. 1:1) in verses 1 through 17. Make a few comments about this passage before moving on to an activity comparing the two narratives of Jesus' birth. A few comments to make are:

- The genealogy begins with Abraham and concludes with Joseph.
- Five women are included in the list, which is very unusual.
- The text says there are fourteen generations between "the deportation to Babylon to the Messiah" (1:17). However, when you count the names, you find only thirteen.
- The genealogy in Matthew is different from the one in Luke.

It will be helpful for you to consult the notes in a study Bible and/or a commentary in order to have sufficient background when you share these comments.

Introduce or review the concept of Synoptic Gospels. Explain that the first three Gospels are called the Synoptic Gospels because "we can see the three Gospels together." This means that many passages in one Gospel have parallel passages in one or two of the other Gospels. This is the case with the narrative of Jesus' birth, which can be found in both Matthew and Luke. This activity of the session plan includes several parts:

- Ask the participants, without looking at the Matthew text, to tell all they can remember about the Matthew passage of the birth of Jesus. That will probably be a confusing task because people tend to view this event as one narrative and are unable to distinguish the differences between the two.
- After members of the group have tried to tell only Matthew's story of Jesus' birth, turn to Matthew 1:18–2:12 to see how much of what they mentioned is correct and what they omitted.
- Divide the class into two smaller groups. One group will work with Matthew and the other with Luke. If your class is larger than twelve members, you could have two or more small groups working with each Gospel.
- Instruct them to turn to page 108, where there is a worksheet titled "Comparing the Birth Narratives." Each group is to answer the ten questions based only on its Gospel. This should not take any longer than ten minutes since the text is limited and the questions are very straightforward.
- After each group has completed the work on its assigned Gospel, the results can be shared in one of three ways: 1. Work as one big group, answering each question for each Gospel and recording the answers on a large chart. 2. Divide into pairs, with Matthew and Luke being represented in each pair. The two persons can share their answers for each question. 3. Divide into small groups of four or six persons, with Matthew and Luke each being represented equally.
- When the members of the group have compared answers, spend a few minutes responding to questions such as: 1. Which of the narratives do you like best? 2. If we had only the Matthew narrative (or Luke), what would you miss that is only in the Luke (or Matthew) narrative? 3. What value is there in being able to distinguish what is in one Gospel compared to what is in another?

The Sermon on the Mount

The Sermon on the Mount is a collection of sayings, or teachings, of Jesus, all presented by the author of Matthew in one sermon or narrative. Invite the participants to turn to Matthew chapters 5 through 7. Call attention to the following elements in the sermon: the Beatitudes (5:1–12); a series of five teachings regarding the law ("You have heard that it was said . . . But I say to you") in chapter 5; three aspects of piety (alms, prayer, fasting) in chapter 6; a series of wise sayings or teachings from 6:19 to the end of chapter 7, and finally the parable about the two houses, one built on sand and the other on rock. Do the following things to help the group review the Sermon on the Mount.

- Divide into three equal-size groups. If you have a group of more than fifteen persons, you many want to subdivide them further in order to have groups that are no larger than four or five persons each.
- Each group will work with a different topic:

  Group 1: Teachings of Jesus regarding the law (5:21–48)

  Group 2: Acts of piety (6:1–18)

  Group 3: Wise sayings (5:13–20 and 6:17–7:20)
- Direct the groups to the worksheet on page 109 for them to use as they work on their part of the Sermon on the Mount.
- Each group will designate a spokesperson to report a summary of the group's findings.
- After the three groups complete their summaries, look at the concluding parable of the Wise and Foolish House Builders. Discuss together the relevance of this parable to all that is presented in the three preceding chapters.

An Overview of Matthew

Take about fifteen minutes to guide the group through an overview of the structure and content of Matthew. You can use the outline presented on pages 21 to 23, which describes a sequence of sections of the book alternating between narratives and discourses. The group has already looked at the genealogy, birth narrative, and the discourse from the mount, so you can begin your overview with chapter 8. The members of the group can follow in their Bibles as you quickly lead them through the book to chapter 28. The goal of this exercise is to highlight the contents of Matthew. An alternative strategy is to copy an outline of the Gospel from a study Bible or commentary and distribute copies of the outline to the participants for them to follow as you guide them through the book. A printed outline will provide them with something they can use later when they want to find something specific in the Gospel.

Practice with Footnotes

Distribute Bibles that are all alike, with footnotes, so that it will be easier to do this activity. You can also check to see how many of the participants have Bibles with footnote references; they could use both Bibles to identify their similarities and differences. Review the examples that are presented on pages 23–24. Then, direct the group to skim in the book of Matthew to find other types of footnotes. As an example, direct them to Matthew 6:13 and the footnote that indicates the source of the added familiar words to the Lord's Prayer. Invite them to share things they find that interest them and to ask questions. Allow about ten minutes for this activity.

Closing

In Matthew 28:18–20 we read Jesus' last words to the disciples, often referred to as "The Great Commission." For the closing of this session, you will use the words as a commissioning of the group members.

You say, "Jesus said, 'Go,'" and the group responds, "We will go."

You say, "Jesus said, 'Make disciples.'" The group responds, "We will make disciples."

You say, "Jesus said, 'Teach.'" The group responds, "We will teach."

You say, "Jesus said, 'And remember, I am with you always.'" The group responds, "We are thankful for Jesus' promise to be with us always."

It will be helpful to write this third response on a sheet of newsprint or chalkboard so that everyone can repeat it. For the other three responses, participants simply repeat the words of Jesus.

Comparing the Birth Narratives

Group 1: Matthew 1:18–2:12	Questions to Answer	Group 2: Luke 2:1–20
1.	Where did Mary and Joseph live?	1.
2.	In what city was Jesus born?	2.
3.	Where in the city was Jesus born?	3.
4.	Why did Mary and Joseph go to Bethlehem?	4.
5.	What ruler is mentioned?	5.
6.	Is a star mentioned?	6.
7.	Are angels mentioned?	7.
8.	Who comes to Bethlehem to visit Jesus?	8.
9.	What do they bring?	9.
10.	What voices of authority are quoted?	10.

The Sermon on the Mount

Introduction: The Sermon on the Mount is presented in chapters 5 through 7 of the Gospel of Matthew. In addition to the Beatitudes in the first twelve verses, the sermon includes Jesus' teachings about the law, acts of piety, and wise sayings.

Directions: Work in a small group with one of the following three topics. Read the suggested verses and then with your fellow small group members answer the related questions.

Group 1: Teachings of Jesus regarding the law (5:21–48)

Five times Jesus says, "You have heard that it was said . . .
But I say to you . . ."

A. What are the five subjects of the law addressed by Jesus?

B. Use cross-reference notes, notes from a study Bible, or a concordance to find a statement in the law of the Old Testament to which Jesus makes reference.

C. How would you interpret Jesus' restatement or interpretation of the traditional law?

Group 2: Acts of piety (6:1–18)

A. There are three acts of piety—what are they?

B. Use cross-reference notes, notes from a study Bible, or a concordance to find a teaching from the law of the Old Testament that emphasizes the same practice.

C. How relevant do you think those practices of piety are for Christians today?

Group 3: Wise sayings (5:13–20 and 6:17–20)

A. Make a list of all the images, metaphors, and concepts Jesus uses to reinforce his teachings.

B. How would you summarize the essence of what Jesus is teaching in these sayings?

Session Three
The Gospel of Mark

BEFORE THE SESSION

Focus of the Session

This session focuses on the Gospel of Mark. You will help the members of your Bible study group to identify some of the major characteristics of Mark and also do a quick overview of the Gospel. This session features a major activity in which participants explore Mark looking for questions Jesus asked and questions asked of Jesus by others. Toward the end of the session, you will work with the skill of comparing a key passage with Matthew and Luke.

Advanced Preparation

- Read the passages suggested in the material for the participants.

- Read an introduction in a study Bible or an article in a Bible handbook or dictionary on the Gospel of Mark.
- Prepare a worksheet following the example on page 113 for the activity in which participants identify questions Jesus asked and questions asked of him.
- Bring some books from your library, the pastor's library, or the church's library to display for the participants to browse. Suggested books include a Bible atlas, a Bible dictionary, a Bible concordance, and other books with information about the Gospels. If you have a book showing the Gospels in a parallel format, that would be a good one to display. By displaying books each week, you will be introducing the participants to some of the resources they may want to purchase for their own libraries if they are motivated to do more in-depth Bible study.

DURING THE SESSION

Welcome of Participants

If there are new participants who did not attend the first two sessions, be sure they are welcomed and briefed regarding what to expect. Greet all of the participants and encourage them to browse among the various translations of the Bible and/or other resources that you have displayed on a table.

Opening Prayer

On page 27 in part 1 you'll find a Prayer Prompted by Scripture activity that features four passages with a brief saying of Jesus. Provide a couple of minutes for persons to select one of the sayings and to write a sentence or two of prayer. It is likely that some in the class will have already completed that activity. If so, they could read through the prayers they wrote in order to select which one they would be willing to share. Or they could write another prayer response or do some editing of one that they have written. After a few minutes, invite the participants to share their brief prayers preceded by their reading the saying of Jesus.

An Overview of the Gospel of Mark

In chapter 3 of the participant's guide, we summarized some of the characteristics of the Gospel of Mark and identified the fact that Mark 8:27–30 is a "hinge" passage separating the two parts of the Gospel. Begin with that passage and share some insights you gained from your reading to help the participants understand the significance of the passage. Discuss with the participants why Jesus might have asked the question, "Who do people say that I am?" (8:27). Then, explain the significance of John the Baptist and Elijah. Continue by commenting on the significance of Peter answering Jesus' second question, "But who do you say that I am?" (8:29). Conclude this part of the discussion with another question for which the participants can share their answers: "Given our own knowledge and experience of Jesus, how would you answer the same question if Jesus were to ask it of you?"

Spend some time sharing with the group members some of what you have learned about Mark from the additional reading you have done or from notes of a previous study of the Gospel. Be sure to include some of the following information:

- Mark is the shortest and first written of the Gospels.
- Matthew and Luke used Mark when they wrote their Gospels.
- John Mark may or may not be the author (explain why).
- Mark is a Gospel of action.

Exploring Questions in Mark

Involve the whole group in exploring the Gospel. Divide the chapters of Mark (but not chapters 13 and 16) among the group so that each person has one or two chapters with which to work. If the group is larger than fourteen, some chapters can be skimmed by more than one person. If the group is fewer than seven, you can select which chapters you would like them to work with. Their task is to skim the assigned chapter(s) to find all of the instances of questions being asked of Jesus by others and for questions that Jesus asked. (The reason we eliminated chapters 13 and 16 is that there are no questions asked in either.) Create a worksheet for them to use to write down what they find using a format like what follows.

After participants have filled in these boxes, take time to have them share their findings. It is not necessary to deal with every question in the whole Gospel, but perhaps focus on one representative question from each of the fourteen chapters. To conclude this activity, ask and discuss one additional question: "What do we learn about Jesus and about the people with whom he exchanged questions and answers?"

Question asked	By whom?	Of whom?	Answer given

The Great Commandment

Beginning on page 32 there is a brief discussion about the passage identified as the Great Commandment. This is another example of a passage that has parallel passages in the other two of the Synoptic Gospels, Matthew and Luke. This activity will engage the participants in a process of comparing the three parallel passages to discover their similarities and differences. The purpose of the activity is to help participants realize that each of the Gospel writers had his own particular intentions for writing what they did, even when they were relating the same event. If there were differences about who Jesus was and what he did among the earliest believers, it should not be surprising that we have differences today about how we understand Jesus. Rather than being disturbed by the differences, we should appreciate the fact that our understanding of Jesus is enhanced when we see the variety of ways he is presented.

Use the worksheet on page 115 to guide this activity. Divide the group into smaller groups of three persons each. Assign each person in each small group a different one of the three passages. They are to read the passage and answer the six questions. After they have answered the questions, each small group of three is to compare their answers, one question at a time. When the groups of three have completed their sharing, spend a few minutes as a whole group reflecting on what they have found. You could guide the discussion with one or more of the following questions:

- What is something you discovered in the comparison that surprised you?

- How would you account for the differences between the three passages?
- Which of the passages do you prefer?
- What is your impression of Jesus' tactics in each of the three passages?

Closing

Before closing the session with prayer, invite the participants to share some of their thoughts about Jesus' approach to persons as he encountered them. On page 30 the participants are invited to complete an activity that identifies many of the encounters Jesus had with individuals and groups. Ask the participants to focus on one of Jesus' encounters and to imagine themselves present in that setting. They are not the principle party of the encounter, but an observer. Ask the question, "As an observer of Jesus' encounter with others, what is a question you would like to ask Jesus?"

Conclude by offering a prayer that expresses your appreciation for Jesus' ministry and his willingness to hear any questions we may have.

The Great Commandment: Comparing Three Gospels

Directions: Work in groups of three. Each person in the small group will work a different one of the three passages. Answer the six questions based only on what you read in your passage. When you have completed all the questions, compare notes to see the similarities and differences between the three Gospels.

	Matthew 22:34–46	**Mark 12:28–34**	**Luke 10:25–42**
1. What is the setting?			
2. Who is present?			
3. Who asks the question about the commandments?			
4. Why does the person ask the question?			
5. Who answers the question?			
6. What happens next?			

Session Four

The Gospel of Luke

BEFORE THE SESSION

Focus of the Session

In this session you will focus on the key events and personalities of the Gospel of Luke. After the opening prayer activity, you will provide a brief overview of some of the distinguishing features of Luke. The opening prayer activity and the activity that follows are directly linked; they focus on the importance of meals and meals with Jesus. As in each session, there will be time to provide an overview of the Gospel of Luke. The specific skill you want participants to practice in this session is working with cross-reference notes.

Advanced Preparation

- Read the passages suggested in the material for the participants.

- Read articles in a Bible dictionary or encyclopedia on the Gospel of Luke.
- One of the features of Luke is all the references to meals. It would be good to plan to have some refreshments that might be representative of the kinds of food persons ate in Jesus' day and still eat today in the Middle East. Foods could include grapes, figs, dates, hummus, pita bread, olives, and grape juice. The food will be used as part of the opening prayer.

DURING THE SESSION

Opening Prayer

Page 44 contains a list of ten passages in Luke where Jesus shared meals with persons. Call attention to the quote from Dr. Culpepper on page 44. If you have arranged for Middle Eastern foods for this session, you could have them either on a buffet table or perhaps some on each table. Remind the participants of the many meals Jesus shared with individuals and groups.

As people are seated at the table(s), invite them to speak about meals they can remember that were very special in their Christian experience. Encourage them to eat the food and drink that has been provided while they are having conversation. If the group is large and there are several tables, each table could have its own conversation. Arrange ahead of time for someone at each table to facilitate the conversation. After five to ten minutes of conversation, interrupt them and ask for individuals to offer brief sentence prayers that express their thanksgiving to God for the bountiful blessings of the fruits of the earth and for the wonderful fellowship that happens when Christians eat together.

Meals with Jesus

After eating together, talking about meals, and offering prayers of thanksgiving, the participants will be ready for this activity, which features meals Jesus shared with individuals and groups. This is intended to be a fifteen-to-twenty-minute activity, but may take longer depending on how involved the participants become in the activity. Consider the following steps in leading the activity:

- How you organize the activity will depend upon how many people are in your group. If you have ten or fewer persons, you could assign a different passage to each person. Or if the group is larger, they could work in small groups, each group with a different passage.

- Direct the participants to page 121, where they will find the worksheet for this activity.
- Assign each person or small group a different passage.
- They are to spend seven to ten minutes reading the passage and answering the questions on the worksheet.
- After ten minutes, when they have completed their exploration, ask the participants to regroup and meet with one or two other persons who worked with different passages.
- In these new, small groups, they are to compare notes.
- After about ten minutes of this sharing, spend a little time as a whole group discussing one additional question: "What do we learn about Jesus from these ten passages that show Jesus sharing meals with others?"

An Overview of the Gospel of Luke

There are a lot of narratives of events, persons, and Jesus' actions and teachings in the twenty-four chapters of Luke. It is impossible to do a quick overview of the Gospel without omitting important things. Therefore, in this part of the session you could do several things to help the participants gain a sense of the whole book. Try not to get sidetracked, but at the same time it is important to be sensitive to questions group members may have.

- Mention briefly the author and dating questions and make the connection between Luke and the Acts of the Apostles.
- Recall the activity that they did in the session on Matthew when they compared the birth-of-Jesus narratives.
- Call attention to the differences between the genealogy in Luke (3:23–28) with that in Matthew (1:2–17).
- Summarize the story line of Luke using the material from pages 36 through 41.

- Look briefly at Jesus in the synagogue in Nazareth at the beginning of his ministry (Luke 4:16–30). Help the participants understand the setting of this event and why what Jesus said about himself and the two quotes from the Hebrew Scriptures would be so upsetting to those who were present.
- Call attention to the activity the participants did in the session on Mark when they compared the three Gospels regarding the passage on the Great Commandment. Point out that in the Luke version the first question was about eternal life and that the narrative concludes with Jesus telling the parable of the Good Samaritan.
- Spend a little time reviewing the long section of the Gospel from 9:51–19:27.
- Direct the participants to pages 40 to 41, section 7, where the passion and resurrection narratives are summarized (22:1–24:53). The metaphor of a "window" through which to view these events is used. The "window" is a focus on the disciples. There is a list of events involving the disciples followed by the suggestion that we, Jesus' disciples today, act in similar ways. Lead the group in a discussion of this. Inquire whether it is a fair analogy to compare Jesus' disciples then with us as his disciples today.

Cross-Reference Notes

The skill we want to work with in this session is the use of cross-reference notes. Not all Bibles have cross-reference notes, so it will be important to either provide such Bibles for everyone or make a photocopy of the page of a Bible with such notes related to Luke 4:1–13. If you cannot find a Bible with cross-reference notes, you could use a study Bible. You must provide references to passages in the Old Testament that Jesus is quoting.

Immediately after Jesus' baptism by John and the list of ancestors, there is a narrative of his time of temptation by the devil in the wilderness. Jesus is tempted three times, and each time he responds to the tempter by quoting a passage from the Hebrew Scriptures. The task is to use the cross-reference notes to locate the passages that Jesus is quoting.

After everyone has found the three passages (Deut. 6:13, 16; 8:3), call the group's attention to the fact that these are words attributed to Moses spoken from Mount Nebo during his last address to the people prior to their entry into the Promised Land. Moses was preparing the people for their new life and mission in a new land across the Jordan. It would be helpful to have a large map to show where Mount Nebo is and where Jesus may have been in the wilderness during the time of his temptation. After this exercise, lead the group in a discussion using questions such as the following:

- Do think that this connection between Moses' words prior to crossing the Jordan and Jesus quoting those words is coincidental or intentional? If intentional, on whose part: Jesus or the writer of Luke, and also Matthew?
- What connections do you see between the setting or situation of the people of Israel prior to beginning a new life in the land across the Jordan and Jesus beginning his ministry?
- How helpful do you think it is to be able to quote Scripture when faced with difficult situations, temptations, and crises?
- What passages of Scripture give you hope, strength, and courage for your daily living?

Closing

The Prayer Prompted by Scripture activity on page 35 includes ten aspects of Jesus' faith and life journey. The readers were invited to read ten brief passages in Luke and to use those ten "steps" of the journey as a basis for reflecting on their own faith and life journeys. Some of the members of your class probably did that exercise. For the closing prayer, ask the participants to turn to page 35 and individually to select one of the "steps" of the journey to be their focus. Ask them to read the brief passage of Luke and then to reflect for a minute or two on the question associated with that passage. After a few minutes, invite the participants to offer brief sentence prayers in response to the particular steps of the journey they have focused on.

Meals with Jesus

Directions: Work individually or with one other person. Select one of the following passages to be the focus of your exploration for this activity. Read the passage and then answer the four questions based on the content of the passage you chose. After you have answered all of the questions, meet with one or two other persons who have explored different passages and compare notes. Work on one question at a time with each of you sharing what you found in your passage.

5:27–32	A meal with Levi after Jesus calls him to be a disciple
7:36–50	A meal with Simon the Pharisee
9:10–17	The feeding of five thousand hungry people
14:1–6	A meal with a leader of the Pharisees on the Sabbath
14:15–24	The parable of the Great Banquet
15:11–32	A meal celebrating the return of the lost son
19:1–10	A meal implied (Jesus is a guest of Zacchaeus)
22:14–23	The Passover meal with the disciples
24:13–31	A meal in which Jesus is recognized in the breaking of the bread
24:36–49	A last meal shared before the ascension of Jesus

Answer the following four questions:

1. With whom is a meal being shared?

____

____

2. What is the occasion of the meal?

____

____

3. What is the significance of the meal?

____

____

2. What happens after the meal?

____

____

Be prepared to share the findings of your passage with others who have explored different passages.

Session Five

The Gospel of John

BEFORE THE SESSION

Focus of the Session

The Gospel of John is different than the other three Gospels, and that will be one of the things you need to emphasize in this session. In addition to the overview of John, there are two major activities. One will focus on two key encounters Jesus had with persons: Nicodemus and the Samaritan woman. The encounters will be dramatized and discussed in order to identify some of the important points of Jesus' ministry and message. The other major activity features names and titles of Jesus. This activity will also help to uncover some of the key aspects of Jesus' ministry and message.

Advanced Preparation

- Read the material in chapter 5 for the participants in part 1.

- Read introductory article(s) on John in one or more study Bibles.
- Read articles in a Bible dictionary or encyclopedia on *logos, names,* and *Messiah.*
- Check passages in a commentary on the Gospel of John regarding the prologue featuring the word *logos* and the phrase *I am.*
- Photocopy brief articles from one or two Bible dictionaries of the names and titles of Jesus that will be used in one of the activities in the session. Each person will need at least one article on one name or title. It would be best if each had two brief articles.

DURING THE SESSION

Opening Prayer

The Prayer Prompted by Scripture activity in chapter 5, page 46, is a litany featuring the six "I am . . ." passages in John. Introduce the litany by reminding the participants of the importance of names in the Old and New Testaments. Call attention to the narrative in Exodus 3 where Moses heard God's call to return to Egypt but had several excuses as to why he could not do that. One of the excuses was he did not know God's name. Then God revealed the divine name as "I AM." When you know a person's name, you know something intimate about the person. When you survey both testaments, you discover there are dozens of names and titles for God. Psalms alone contains more than thirty names, titles, or images used by the writer to identify God. The same is true in the New Testament and particularly in the Gospel of John, where we find many names, titles, and images for Jesus. A later activity in the session will involve the participants in exploring nine names and titles for Jesus.

For the opening prayer, invite the persons to turn to page 46 and to pray responsively this litany on the "I am . . ." passages. Either the leader or another member of the group will read the words of Jesus, and the rest of the group will pray the response in unison. After you have completed the prayer, spend a few minutes discussing the following questions:

- When you consider all six images Jesus uses to identify himself, how would you summarize what you learn about Jesus?

- Which of the images of Jesus speaks most significantly to you? Why?
- If Jesus were to speak to a group of Christians today and were to use some images from our culture and experience, what might he say to complete the sentence "I am . . ."?

An Overview of the Gospel of John

There is a lot of content to deal with as you help the participants gain an overview of the Gospel of John. Your goal is to help them be aware of some of the questions regarding authorship and date and to gain a sense of the unique features of John. To provide an overview, you may find it helpful to address the following topics. Be careful not to make the whole session a lecture; it is important to leave enough time for two activities that are described below.

- Based on your reading, offer a few comments regarding the questions of authorship and dating of the Gospel.
- Call attention to some or all of the key features of the Gospel, making reference to the six topics that are presented beginning on page 50. You may want to have the participants look at some specific passages that illustrate the key features that you present.
- Refer the group to page 18 where there is a chart showing the number of chapters in each of the four Gospels devoted to the four parts of the life, ministry, death, and resurrection of Jesus. Make note that almost one-half (ten of twenty-one chapters) of John is devoted to the passion and resurrection parts of the story. Mark devotes about the same percentage of the book to the same parts of the story, whereas Matthew and Luke devote a much smaller percentage.
- Invite the participants to take about five minutes to skim through the Gospel and to select one or two verses or one narrative that is either their favorite or that speaks to them in a special way. Take a few minutes for participants to share what they have selected. If you have a group larger than a dozen, you may want them to do this sharing in smaller groups.

Two Key Persons: Nicodemus and the Samaritan Woman

We have already indicated that there are two particular narratives involving two individuals in an extended dialogue with Jesus. These are the narratives involving Nicodemus and the Samaritan woman. If you have sufficient time, work with both of the narratives. If you don't have enough time, choose to work with just one. On page 128 you will find a dramatized reading for the dialogue between Jesus and Nicodemus, and on pages 129–130 you will find a reading of the dialogue between Jesus and the Samaritan woman. Whether you work with both narratives or just one, use the following steps to involve the participants:

- Ask for volunteers for the several parts in each of the dialogues. You will need participants to read the narrator and Jesus parts in the Nicodemus dialogue, and you will need volunteers for the narrator, Jesus, disciples, and people parts in the Samaritan woman dialogue. The whole group will read in unison the Nicodemus and the woman parts. There are two reasons for having the participants read these two parts: 1. Through this method everyone is involved. 2. The participants have the opportunity to identify with the key character in each story.
- If you use both dialogues, work with one and follow it up with a discussion, and then do the same with the second dialogue.
- After each dialogue, you can lead the discussion with questions such as these:

  What do we learn about Jesus in this dialogue? (Be sure to emphasize that Jesus reaches out to people you would have expected him to avoid—a Pharisee and a Samaritan, a woman no less.)

  What do we learn about the other person? (Emphasize that both Nicodemus and the woman were more than curious about Jesus; they desired very much to learn from Jesus.)

  Why do you think John 3:16 is one of the most often quoted verses in the Bible?

  What do you think about when you hear or speak the words "eternal life"?

Jesus speaks to the woman about "living water" and "worship in spirit and truth." What is the meaning of those concepts in the context of the dialogue and also in the context of Christian faith and life today?

Names and Titles of Jesus in John

In all four Gospels there are many names, titles, and images used to identify Jesus. On page 52 we list nine different ways of identifying Jesus. This activity will involve group members in exploring these nine key words. The following suggestions will help you guide the activity:

- Direct the participants to the worksheet on page 131.
- Divide the nine names and titles for Jesus among the members of the group. If you have fewer than nine in your group, select which of the nine you want them to work with, or just let each person choose a different one. If you have more than nine members, encourage participants to work in pairs.
- Give to each person or group the brief articles you have photocopied from a Bible dictionary or wordbook for their assigned words.
- Provide about fifteen to twenty minutes for them to read the article and the material in the participant's section of this book and to answer the questions.
- After allowing time for exploring the available material and finding at least one Bible passage, ask the participants to join with another person (or two) who has worked on different words.
- In these small groups, they are to share what they have discovered about their key words.
- After allowing time for sharing in the small groups, spend a few minutes with the whole group responding to one additional question: "What have we learned about Jesus from this exploration of the nine key names, titles, or images used to identify him?"

Closing

You probably will not have very much time to spare at the end of this session. This suggestion for a closing prayer can be accomplished in two to three minutes. Invite participants to complete a sentence that begins with the word "Jesus." The participants take a half-minute to write down a sentence completion or to think of one. Then, invite the members to share their sentences. Following each sentence the whole group speaks in unison with the response, "O God, help me to follow Jesus wherever he leads me."

Jesus and Nicodemus

(John 3:1–2, NRSV)

Narrator: Now there was a Pharisee named Nicodemus, a leader of the Jews. He came to Jesus by night and said to him,

Nicodemus: Rabbi, we know that you are a teacher who has come from God; for no one can do these signs that you do apart from the presence of God.

Jesus: Very truly, I tell you, no one can see the kingdom of God without being born from above.

Nicodemus: How can anyone be born after having grown old? Can one enter a second time into the mother's womb and be born?

Jesus: Very truly, I tell you, no one can enter the kingdom of God without being born of water and Spirit. What is born of the flesh is flesh, and what is born of the Spirit is spirit. Do not be astonished that I said to you, "You must be born from above." The wind blows where it chooses, and you hear the sound of it, but you do not know where it comes from or where it goes. So it is with everyone who is born of the Spirit.

Nicodemus: How can these things be?

Jesus: Are you a teacher of Israel, and yet you do not understand these things? Very truly, I tell you, we speak of what we know and testify to what we have seen; yet you do not receive our testimony. If I have told you about earthly things and you do not believe, how can you believe if I tell you about heavenly things? No one has ascended into heaven except the one who descended from heaven, the Son of Man. And just as Moses lifted up the serpent in the wilderness, so must the Son of Man be lifted up, that whoever believes in him may have eternal life. For God so loved the world that he gave his only Son, so that everyone who believes in him may not perish but may have eternal life. Indeed, God did not send the Son into the world to condemn the world, but in order that the world might be saved through him. Those who believe in him are not condemned; but those who do not believe are condemned already, because they have not believed in the name of the only Son of God. And this is the judgment, that the light has come into the world, and people loved darkness rather than light because their deeds were evil. For all who do evil hate the light and do not come to the light, so that their deeds may not be exposed. But those who do what is true come to the light, so that it may be clearly seen that their deeds have been done in God.

Jesus and the Samaritan Woman

(John 4:1–42, NRSV)

Narrator:	Now when Jesus learned that the Pharisees had heard, "Jesus is making and baptizing more disciples than John"—although it was not Jesus himself but his disciples who baptized—he left Judea and started back to Galilee. But he had to go through Samaria. So he came to a Samaritan city called Sychar, near the plot of ground that Jacob had given to his son Joseph. Jacob's well was there, and Jesus, tired out by his journey, was sitting by the well. It was about noon. A Samaritan woman came to draw water, and Jesus said to her,
Jesus:	Give me a drink.
Narrator:	His disciples had gone to the city to buy food. The Samaritan woman said to him,
Woman:	How is it that you, a Jew, ask a drink of me, a woman of Samaria?
Narrator:	Jews do not share things in common with Samaritans.
Jesus:	If you knew the gift of God, and who it is that is saying to you, "Give me a drink," you would have asked him, and he would have given you living water.
Woman:	Sir, you have no bucket, and the well is deep. Where do you get that living water? Are you greater than our ancestor Jacob, who gave us the well, and with his sons and his flocks drank from it?
Jesus:	Everyone who drinks of this water will be thirsty again, but those who drink of the water that I will give them will never be thirsty. The water that I will give will become in them a spring of water gushing up to eternal life.
Woman:	Sir, give me this water, so that I may never be thirsty or have to keep coming here to draw water.
Jesus:	Go, call your husband, and come back.
Woman:	I have no husband.
Jesus:	You are right in saying, "I have no husband"; for you have had five husbands, and the one you have now is not your husband. What you have said is true!
Woman:	Sir, I see that you are a prophet. Our ancestors worshiped on this mountain, but you say that the place where people must worship is in Jerusalem.
Jesus:	Woman, believe me, the hour is coming when you will worship the Father neither on this mountain nor in Jerusalem. You worship what you do not know; we worship what we know, for salvation is from the Jews. But the hour is coming, and is now here, when the true

Jesus and the Samaritan Woman *(continued)*

	worshipers will worship the Father in spirit and truth, for the Father seeks such as these to worship him. God is spirit, and those who worship him must worship in spirit and truth.
Woman:	I know that Messiah is coming (who is called Christ). When he comes, he will proclaim all things to us.
Jesus:	I am he, the one who is speaking to you.
Narrator:	Just then his disciples came. They were astonished that he was speaking with a woman, but no one said, "What do you want?" or, "Why are you speaking with her?" Then the woman left her water jar and went back to the city. She said to the people,
Woman:	Come and see a man who told me everything I have ever done! He cannot be the Messiah, can he?
Narrator:	They left the city and were on their way to him. Meanwhile the disciples were urging him,
Disciples:	Rabbi, eat something.
Jesus:	I have food to eat that you do not know about.
Disciples:	Surely no one has brought him something to eat?
Jesus:	My food is to do the will of him who sent me and to complete his work. Do you not say, "Four months more, then comes the harvest"? But I tell you, look around you, and see how the fields are ripe for harvesting. The reaper is already receiving wages and is gathering fruit for eternal life, so that sower and reaper may rejoice together. For here the saying holds true, "One sows and another reaps." I sent you to reap that for which you did not labor. Others have labored, and you have entered into their labor.
Narrator:	Many Samaritans from that city believed in him because of the woman's testimony, "He told me everything I have ever done." So when the Samaritans came to him, they asked him to stay with them; and he stayed there two days. And many more believed because of his word.
People:	It is no longer because of what you said that we believe, for we have heard for ourselves, and we know that this is truly the Savior of the world.

Names and Titles of Jesus

Directions: Either by yourself or with another person, work with one of the following key names, titles, or images of Jesus. Read the brief articles that are provided related to your word or phrase. Read the description in the participant's section of this book, and check out the recommended passages in order to select one or two passages that are helpful in understanding this name or title of Jesus.

Names and Titles of Jesus

Jesus	Word	Lamb of God
Rabbi	Messiah	Savior
King	Lord	Son of Joseph and Jesus of Nazareth

Questions to Explore

1. How often is Jesus called by this name?

2. What is the context in which he is called by this name?

3. What, if any, are the Old Testament connections to the name?

4. What do we learn of the nature of Jesus' life and ministry from this name?

5. What relevance is there to this name of Jesus for thinking or speaking about him today?

Session Six

The Acts of the Apostles

BEFORE THE SESSION

Focus of the Session

We have a big task ahead of us in this session as we move through the many chapters of the book of Acts. Many persons, events, issues, and conflicts are presented in these twenty-eight chapters. It would be worth spending a whole course of six to ten weeks on Acts. However, in this session the best you can do is provide an overview and identify some of the highlights of the book. The major activity focuses on Paul's four journeys. There is also a brief activity that helps the participants make connections between what they are reading in Acts with the life and ministry of their own church.

Advanced Preparation

- Read the passages in the material suggested for the participants.

- Read articles in a Bible dictionary or encyclopedia or in a study Bible about the book of Acts.
- If you don't have enough time to read the whole book of Acts, it is important to skim the whole book so that you will have a sense of the structure and flow of the story line.
- Provide a large map that shows the area of Paul's four journeys. Or, if you have access to a resource that has smaller maps that you can photocopy, provide a map for each participant.

DURING THE SESSION

Opening Prayer

The opening prayer for this session is a prayer of the believers in Jerusalem after Peter and John had been released following their trial before the authorities for healing a man and preaching that Jesus was the Messiah, raised from the dead. Follow these suggested steps for leading the group in this opening prayer:

- Set the stage by reviewing the events in Acts 3:1–4:22. Be sure to have the group look closely at 4:1–22. Beginning at 4:24b is the prayer of the people.
- Lead the group in praying this prayer in unison using the words of the Contemporary English Version on page 137.
- After the prayer, allow for about a minute of silence for persons to continue praying in their own words.
- Conclude by reading, "After they had prayed, the meeting place shook. They were all filled with the Holy Spirit and bravely spoke God's message" (4:31 CEV).

An Overview of the Book of Acts of the Apostles

The story of the Christian church's earliest days is composed of many events and persons. It is a dynamic, dramatic, and compelling story. It is a story worthy of a whole course, and that might be something you and your group would want to do at a later time. In this session the best you can do is call attention to some of the highlights of the story because you want to leave time for the two activities that follow. As you provide an overview of the book of Acts, you will want to include some or all of the following points based on what you have learned in your reading:

- Refer to the authorship and dating of the book and that this is a second volume attributed to Luke, addressed to Theophilus.
- Provide a large map for the whole group to see, or reproduce a smaller map so that everyone has a map in front of him or her. Use the references from Acts on page 65 to help the participants see how the good news spread from Jerusalem to Rome. Be sure that the map shows all of the places mentioned in these passages.
- The good news spread because the disciples were faithful in their witness to Jesus as the risen Messiah, and many who heard responded by believing this good news. Summarize the points made in the section "A Spirit-Led Church" beginning on page 61.
- A direct result of the work of the Holy Spirit is that many were blessed by the Holy Spirit, were converted, and believed. Call attention to several of the conversion experiences of crowds and individuals that are outlined on page 66.
- One of the critical factors contributing to the growth of the early church was the gift of the Holy Spirit to the Gentiles as well as to the Jews. This was also a critical issue faced by the church; the leaders had to decide whether Gentiles could be received into their fellowship without having to observe all the requirements and traditions of the law of Moses. Comment on both Peter's and Paul's role in this issue and on the Council in Jerusalem (15:1–35).
- Another factor contributing to the growth of the church was the outreach by Paul and his companions and the three journeys they conducted. It is not necessary to develop this point because that will be explored in one of the activities that follow.

The Life and Ministry of the Church

In this part of the session, we want to identify those activities of the early church that contributed to their growth and characterized their life together. This is not an extended activity but one that you can do with the whole group (or participants can do in smaller groups). On page 138 is a list of passages. Read them one at a time. Either on a sheet of newsprint for the whole group or on worksheets for small groups, write down all of the church's activities of ministry and church members' life together that are mentioned or alluded to in the several passages. After recording all of the activities, spend some time discussing ministries of your own church that are similar to those activities of ministry of the early church as described in Acts. Try not to spend more than fifteen minutes on this activity. When you have completed the task, briefly discuss these questions:

- If these were activities that contributed to the early church's growth, how will or do similar activities contribute to our church's growth today?
- What else do we need to do to help our church spread the good news of Jesus Christ?

The Four Journeys of Paul

This is the major participatory activity of the session. Introduce the activity by speaking about the importance of Paul's ministry in the formation of the early church. As you guide the participants in this activity, keep the following things in mind:

- If your class has from four to sixteen participants, you could divide them into four small groups and ask each group to explore one of the four journeys. If your group consists of more than sixteen people, you may want to have more than one group working on the same journeys.
- There are a lot of verses to read for each journey. To accomplish the tasks without taking too much time, suggest to the small groups that they divide the passages of their journey among the members of the group so that each person is reading or skimming a smaller portion of the total text.

- Remind the groups that they are not preparing a comprehensive report of the journey but that they are trying to gain an *overview* of the journey. Therefore, they should work as quickly as possible.
- It would be helpful for each group to work at separate tables.
- After the small groups have completed their work (which should take about twenty minutes), ask each person in a group to join with three others, each of whom has explored a different journey. In these new small groups, they are to take about fifteen minutes to compare notes on what they discovered.

Closing

Conclude by offering a prayer of thanksgiving. Ask each person to think of one or more persons who have been instrumental in her or his faith formation and spiritual nurture, persons who have shared with them the good news of the gospel of Jesus Christ. Invite them, one at a time, to name such an individual. After each person has offered a name, the whole group will respond in unison, "Thanks be to God for this faithful witness."

The Believers' Prayer

"Master, you created heaven and earth, the sea, and everything in them. And by the Holy Spirit you spoke to our ancestor David. He was your servant, and you told him to say:

'Why are all the Gentiles so furious?
  Why do people make foolish plans?
The kings of earth prepare for war,
and the rulers join together against the Lord and his Messiah.'

Here in Jerusalem, Herod and Pontius Pilate got together with the Gentiles and the people of Israel. Then they turned against your holy Servant Jesus, your chosen Messiah. They did what you in your power and wisdom had already decided would happen.

Lord, listen to their threats! We are your servants. So make us brave enough to speak your message. Show your mighty power, as we heal people and work miracles and wonders in the name of your holy Servant, Jesus. [Amen.]"

(Acts 4:24b–30 CEV)

The Life and Ministry of the Church

Read the following passages: Acts 2:2–47; 4:13–22; 4:32–37; and 6:1–7.

In the first column, list all the activities that are mentioned or alluded to in these passages that give clues to the nature of members' life together in the early church. Then, list in the second column the activities in your church that are illustrative of these same activities of the early church.

Activities of the Church in Acts	Similar Activities in Our Church Today
______________________________	______________________________
______________________________	______________________________
______________________________	______________________________
______________________________	______________________________
______________________________	______________________________
______________________________	______________________________
______________________________	______________________________
______________________________	______________________________

The Four Journeys of Paul

Directions: Work with a small group. Your group will work with one of the four journeys of Paul and his companions. Read the assigned passage and then answer the questions that are listed below. Take about twenty minutes to explore your passage. When you have completed the task, you will meet with individuals who explored the other three journeys to compare notes.

Four Journeys of Paul

Group 1	First Missionary Journey	Acts 13:1–14:28
Group 2	Second Missionary Journey	Acts 15:36–18:22
Group 3	Third Missionary Journey	Acts 18:23–21:8
Group 4	The Journey to Rome	Acts 27:1–28:31

Questions to Explore

1. Who were Paul's companions on the journey?

2. What cities or geographical sites did they visit?

3. What were some of the important events or encounters of the journey?

4. What were some of the major accomplishments of the journey?

Session Seven
Epistles of the New Testament

BEFORE THE SESSION

Focus of the Session

In this session, we cover about four-fifths of the books of the New Testament. Obviously we cannot do justice to all of the content of the books that are identified as epistles or letters. However, we can deal with some or all of the epistles in a general way so that the participants will be introduced to this collection and will feel more comfortable returning to one or more of the epistles to read and/or study them in more depth. In this session, we spend a little time reviewing the life and ministry of the apostle Paul. Paul is a key figure in the New Testament, and many of the epistles are attributed to him. We were not able to spend much time exploring Paul in the previous chapter, so we will get a little better acquainted with him now. The major activity of this session will be providing the opportunity for each member of the group to explore one of the epistles.

Advanced Preparation

- Read the passages in the material suggested for the participants.
- Read brief articles in a Bible dictionary or encyclopedia and a study Bible on the general category of "epistles in the New Testament."
- It would be helpful to have a map of the New Testament world to refer to when identifying some of the cities to which letters were written.
- Photocopy brief articles from a study Bible, a Bible dictionary, and/or a Bible encyclopedia for each of the epistles that will be featured in the major activity on exploring the epistles. Each person will work with one epistle, and it would be helpful for each to have one or two short articles that provide an introduction to the book he or she is exploring.
- Photocopy the worksheet on page 146 for each member of the class. Prior to the class session, print the name of one of the epistles on each sheet.

DURING THE SESSION

Opening Prayer

Three of the epistles contain passages that speak of particular gifts of the Spirit that are given to those who follow in the way of Jesus Christ. The passages are Romans 12:6–8; 1 Corinthians 12:4–7, 27–31; and Ephesians 4:11–13. There are a variety of gifts. Every believer is blessed with particular gifts. No one believer has all of the gifts, and no two believers have identical gifts. The gifts are given to individuals for the benefit of the whole body, the church. This opening prayer is in the form of a litany that is found on page 145. Ask the participants to turn to the litany, "Gifts of God for the People of God." Call attention to the last statement, where there is no printed prayer response. Tell the group that after the last statement is read, there will be a brief period of silence for participants to write or think of a sentence prayer response. Afterward, you will read the statement again and invite members to share their own brief prayers. After praying the litany, spend a few minutes discussing the biblical concept of gifts with a question or two:

- What do you think are some differences between gifts, talents, and skills?
- Of the eight gifts mentioned in the litany, with which one or two do you think you have been blessed by God?
- How are you using your gifts in the service of God and God's people?
- Is it hard or easy to see ourselves as having gifts, or being gifted? Why?
- What are some ways we can affirm the gifts of others?

The Apostle Paul: Missionary and Prolific Writer

As we mentioned earlier, Paul is a very important person in the formation of the early church. He is featured in the book of Acts from chapter 9 to the end. In chapter 6 of this study, we focused only on Paul's journeys and not on him as a person. Since he is believed to have been the author of many of the epistles, we are going to spend a little time getting better acquainted with the apostle Paul. Before proceeding with the activity, call attention to two passages: 1. Paul (Saul) was present at the killing of Stephen (Acts 8:10), and 2. Paul includes himself among the apostles, though he sees himself as the least of them (1 Cor. 15:1–11).

There are three extended passages where Paul tells of his life before Christ, his conversion, and his ministry in the name of Christ: Acts 21:37–22:21; Acts 26:1–23; and Galatians 1:11–2:21. In each passage, Paul is defending himself by telling about his life and ministry. The activity should take about fifteen minutes. Guide the group through the following steps:

- Divide the large group into groups of three.
- Assign each person in the group one of the three passages.
- Each person is to read her or his assigned passage and then list phrases that are descriptive of Paul as a person and of his ministry.
- When they have finished reading and making their list, the small groups of three are to compare notes to see the similarities and differences between their descriptive phrases.
- An alternative strategy would be to divide the whole

group by thirds, assigning each third one of the passages and then comparing notes as a whole group.

Exploring an Epistle

Introduce this activity by first presenting some general information about the genre of epistles in the New Testament, based on your additional reading in preparation for the session. Be sure to make note of three types of epistles: those written to individuals, those written to churches, and those written to a general group of believers. Also, underscore the point that even though many of the books are attributed to Paul there is doubt among Bible scholars as to the authenticity of his authorship of some of the letters. You might want to mention that Revelation is also written as a letter to seven churches but that it is a very different type of literature and will be dealt with in session 8.

This activity will take about thirty to forty minutes. Lead the group through the activity with these steps:

- You could ask for volunteers or assign one letter to each person. If you have more than twenty-one people in your class, you could assign two members to the longer, more complicated letters.
- Distribute the worksheets you have duplicated as well as the brief articles associated with the particular letters.
- The participants should be able to complete the task of reading a brief article or two and answering the questions on the worksheet in about twenty minutes.
- When the participants have completed answering the questions on the worksheets, gather as a whole group so that each person can make a brief presentation about her or his epistle. Remind them not to share the key passage they have selected because that will be done as part of the closing.
- Another strategy you could use is to limit the number of letters you will deal with and assign small groups of two to four persons to work together on the selected epistles. It would be a good idea for each person in the small group to have a different brief article about the letter. After participants complete their reading, they could work together to answer the questions on the worksheet.

Closing

The last question/task on the worksheet for exploring an epistle is to select a passage with one to six verses that speaks in a special way to the one who was exploring the letter. For the closing, invite participants to read their verses if they so desire. And, if they would like to share why they chose the passage or why it spoke to them in a special way, they could add that as well.

Gifts of God for the People of God

Leader: Some are gifted as **prophets.**

People: *Help us, O God, to proclaim your Word with wisdom and clarity.*

L. Some are gifted to be of **service** to others.

P. *You have called us to ministry; help us to be faithful in our service.*

L. Some are gifted as **pastors** who minister to God's people.

P. *Loving God, may we minister to your people with love and understanding.*

L. Some are gifted as **teachers.**

P. *We learn from the Master Teacher and seek to teach your way and truth to those whom we serve.*

L. Some are gifted as **encouragers.**

P. *O God, help us to be supportive of others in their spiritual journeys.*

L. Some are gifted with resources for **giving.**

P. *You have blessed us with so much and we are grateful to be able to share our resources with others.*

L. Some are gifted as **leaders.**

P. *Empower us, O God, to be able to guide others with energy and vision.*

L. Some are gifted with the ability to be **compassionate.**

P. *Dear God, may we show empathy and kindness in your name.*

L. All of us are gifted by the Holy Spirit to serve God and to serve others in God's name.

P. *O God . . .*

Exploring an Epistle

Directions: You will spend about twenty minutes exploring the epistle named on this sheet. Read the two brief articles about the epistle given to you. Then quickly answer the questions below. When you have completed the tasks, prepare to make a very brief presentation to the whole group.

Epistle ______________________

To whom is the letter addressed?

If the writer is identified, who is it?

What is the approximate date of writing?

If a reason is given for writing the letter, what is it?

What is a major theme or emphasis of the writer of this epistle?

What is one key passage (of one to six verses) that speaks to you in a special way?

Session Eight
The Revelation to John

BEFORE THE SESSION

Focus of the Session

We come to the last session of a Bible study that has attempted to provide an introduction to the New Testament for the members of your group. I trust it has been a challenging and satisfying study for you, the leader, as well as for those whom you have led. There is a lot to cover in this session, and if you have the time you may want to take two sessions to complete all of the suggested activities. In this session, we want to gain a sense of the structure, content, and style of The Revelation to John; to attempt to decode some of the symbols; to use our imaginations as we try to visualize the visions of the writer; and to bring closure to the session and the course.

Advanced Preparation

- Read the passages in the material suggested for the participants.

- Read an introductory article in a study Bible about Revelation.
- Read articles in a Bible dictionary or encyclopedia on these key words: *the book of Revelation*, *revelation*, *apocalyptic*, *numbers*, *symbols*, and *the beast*.

DURING THE SESSION

Opening Prayer

Ask the participants to turn to page 78, where there is a series of verses that are in the form of prayers. Each person is to read the prayer verses and to select one that is meaningful to him or her at that moment. Invite them to share their selected verses one at a time. After each has shared, the whole group will say in unison a litany response: "Salvation and power and glory to our God" (19:1). Write this response on a sheet of newsprint or on the white board for the participants. Remind them that it is okay to repeat a line or verse that someone else has shared.

Introducing The Revelation to John

As we have already noted, Revelation is a very complex, confusing, and mysterious book. The best we can do in this session is to help the participants "get their feet wet" in Revelation. In this part of the session, you want to touch on some of the key features and highlights of The Revelation to John. Here are some things you might consider emphasizing:

- Remind your group that the name of the book is Revelation, not Revelations. Using the plural is a common mistake. During the session, if anyone speaks of Revelations it would be helpful to correct the person in a way that he or she is not embarrassed.
- Spend a little bit of time on the issues of authorship, dating, and setting of Revelation. You will need to do some extra reading in a Bible commentary, dictionary, or encyclopedia in order to feel comfortable with the information related to these issues.
- It is important to spend some time explaining the concept of apocalypse and the nature of apocalyptic litera-

ture. To read Revelation with any understanding at all, it is necessary to read the book differently than one reads any other book in the Bible. This will set the stage for the activity on the Visions and the Seven Seals, where you will try to decode some of the images.

- As an example of an apocalyptic vision, read to the group "A Coded Scenario" on page 155. Ask if any in the group have figured out the meanings of the symbols/images, the setting in which it might have been written, and the audience who might have received it. We hope it is clear that the mother eagle represents England and the thirteen little chicks are the original thirteen colonies.
- You may want to restate what is in the participant's section of this book regarding John Wick Bowman's suggestion of reading Revelation as a drama. You could refer to pages 153–154 and the outline of the book in eight acts with a prologue and epilogue.
- With this as background information, tell the group members that they are going to do two or three activities before concluding the session and the course. (If you are limited to one session of one hour or less, you will need to choose which of the three activities you will have time for, along with the closing activity.)

The Seven Churches

Act 1 presents John's letters to seven churches. Introduce the activity by using a map to call attention to the geographical locations of the seven churches. These were real living churches with which John was familiar. It is very possible the whole book of Revelation is addressed to these churches, as John indicates in 1:4. The purpose of this activity is to discover something about each of the churches. John uses a "template" for the seven letters in that all of them follow the same pattern. If you have to omit an activity, this may be the one since the same material is summarized in the participant's material in chapter 8. The steps of the activity are:

- Divide the group into seven smaller groups.
- Direct participants to the worksheet on page 156.

- Assign each group one of the churches to explore.
- They are to read the passage related to the church.
- They are to write just key words and phrases to fill in the blanks for their church.
- This should take about ten minutes. Conclude the activity by quickly receiving reports from each church regarding the five elements of the letters. Work with one element at a time.

Visions and the Seven Seals

There are two things to do in this activity. The first is to try to express visually the symbols/images of Act 2 (Rev. 4:1–8:5). The second is to work at decoding the many symbols/images in this section. Here are some possibilities for presenting the symbols/images visually:

- If you, someone in your group, or a member of the church has the gift of portraying abstract things in a graphic, ask him or her to create a large poster to portray the stage setting of this act. If you had a poster with objects to point to, you would be able identify the objects as you or someone else reads the passage.
- If you have access to books or art and religious objects, you may be able to find visual expressions of this material.
- You could provide construction paper and felt markers of a variety of colors so that members of the group could illustrate their interpretation of the symbols/images. They could do this individually or in small groups of two or three. Remind the participants that their imaginations are the best resource they have for doing this.

After viewing graphic interpretations of these visions, spend some time with the group identifying the meaning of the various symbols/images. There is a chart on page 84 that provides the decoding necessary. After reviewing the chart, invite the participants to reread part of the text to try their hand at interpreting the vision. When you know the meaning of the symbols/images, ask what the meaning is of the message John writes.

All Things New

On page 157 there is a worksheet titled "All Things New." Guide the participants through this activity. It should take no more than ten to fifteen minutes since the passages are relatively short and the three questions are very manageable. The participants can work either by themselves or with another person or two. Spend just a few minutes summarizing what they have discovered in these passages. When they have finished exploring the seven passages from the Old and New Testaments regarding "something new," go to Revelation 21:1–8. Read the passage and then ask the participants, "What insights do you gain from this passage in light of the other passages you have explored?"

Closing

Before moving to the closing prayer, invite the participants to share some of their learnings, insights, observations, and/or experiences regarding their study of the New Testament during the past seven weeks. This is not intended to be a formal evaluation of the course but rather a time for reflecting on and sharing the benefits that have come to the members of the group. You could guide this time of reflection with one or two questions, such as:

- What are your impressions of the New Testament now compared to when we started our study eight weeks ago?
- What has meant the most to you in this time of study?
- Which book or books of the New Testament would you like to return to for further reading and study?
- What Bible or Bible resource would you like to add to your "I'd like to have" list?
- How comfortable do you think you will be to join another Bible study group?
- There is a second course in the series. Would you be interested in being in a Bible study group focusing on *The Bible from Scratch: The Old Testament for Beginners*?

The closing prayer is a hymn. Provide hymnals or the words of one of the following hymns: "Holy, Holy, Holy," "All Hail the Power of Jesus' Name," "Be Thou My Vision," or "The Church's One Foundation." You may be able to sing without accompaniment if the hymn is familiar to the members of the group. If not, and there is no piano or pianist available, you could sing along with a recorded version of the hymn.

An alternative closing would be to ask the participants to complete a sentence that begins with the phrase, "Studying the New Testament . . ." After thirty seconds or so, invite people to share their sentences. After each has spoken, the group should respond in unison: "Dear God, thank you for revealing yourself to us through your Word."

Outline of The Revelation to John

Prologue 1:1–3

Act One Letters to Seven Churches 1:4–3:22

	Introduction	1:4–20
1.	Ephesus	2:1–7
2.	Smyrna	2:8–11
3.	Pergamum	2:12–17
4.	Thyatira	2:18–29
5.	Sardis	3:1–6
6.	Philadelphia	3:7–13
7.	Laodicea	3:14–22

Act Two Visions and Seven Seals 4:1–8:6

	Introduction: The throne, the scroll, and the Lamb	4:1–5:14
1.	First seal—a white horse	6:1–2
2.	Second seal—a red horse	6:3–4
3.	Third seal—a black horse	6:5–6
4.	Fourth seal—a pale green horse	6:7–8
5.	Fifth seal—lament of martyrs	6:9–11
6.	Sixth seal—great earthquake	6:12–17
	Interlude: Sealing of martyrs and glorified martyrs	7:1–17
7.	Seventh seal—silence in heaven	8:1–6

Act Three Seven Angels with Trumpet Woes 8:7–11:19

1.	First trumpet—hail and fire	8:7
2.	Second trumpet—burning mountain falls into the sea	8:8–9
3.	Third trumpet—blazing star falls into the sea	8:10–11
4.	Fourth trumpet—darkening of sun, moon, and stars	8:12
	Interlude: Eagles' warning	8:13
5.	Fifth trumpet—demonic locusts	9:1–12
6.	Sixth trumpet—destroying horsemen from Euphrates	9:13–21
	Interlude: John eats scroll and two heavenly witnesses	10:1–11:14
7.	Seventh trumpet—judgments and rewards	11:15–19

Act Four Seven Visions of Dragon's Kingdom 12:1–13:18

1.	The heavenly mother and the birth of the Messiah	12:1–6
2.	Michael's victory over the dragon	12:7–9
3.	Song of woe and rejoicing	12:10–12
4.	The woman and other children	12:13–13:1
5.	The beast from the sea	13:2–4
6.	The beast's authority	13:5–10
7.	The beast from the earth	13:11–18

From *The First Christian Drama—The Book of Revelation*, John Wick Bowman (Philadelphia: Westminster Press, 1968), originally *The Drama of the Book of Revelation*, 1955.

Outline of The Revelation to John *(continued)*

Act Five	Seven Visions of Worshipers of the Lamb and of the Beast	14:1–20
1.	Martyrs and the Lamb on Mount Zion	14:1–5
2.	The angel's advice to worship God	14:6–7
3.	The angel pronounces doom to Babylon	14:8
4.	The angel condemns worshipers of the beast	14:9–11
5.	The benediction of martyrs	14:12–13
6.	The Son of Man and harvest	14:14–16
7.	The angel and gathering the vintage of the earth	14:17–20
Act Six	Seven Visions of Angels with Bowls of God's Wrath	15:1–16:21
	Preparation	15:1–16:1
1.	Plague of ulcers	16:2
2.	Sea turned to blood	16:3
3.	Rivers and springs turned to blood	16:4–7
4.	Scorching heat of the sun	16:8–9
5.	Darkness of the beast's kingdom	16:10–11
6.	Kings assemble for Armageddon	16:12–16
7.	The impending destruction of Babylon	16:17–21
Act Seven	Seven Visions of the Fall of "Babylon" (or Rome)	17:1–19:10
1.	Prostitute—Babylon the Great	17:1–6
2.	Interpretation of the prostitute and the beast	17:7–18
3.	Proclamation of the fall of Rome	18:1–10
4.	Exultation and mourning over the fall of Rome	18:11–20
5.	The millstone thrown into sea and dirge over the city	18:21–24
6.	The hymn of praise to God	19:1–5
7.	The marriage hymn to the Lamb and his bride	19:6–10
Act Eight	Seven Visions of the End of Satan's Reign/ Beginning of God's Reign	19:11–21:8
1.	The conquering Christ	19:11–16
2.	The victory of Christ over the beast and the antichrist	19:17–21
3.	Satan bound and his rule suspended for one thousand years	20:1–3
4.	The reign of Christ for one thousand years	20: 4–6
5.	Satan cast into the lake of fire	20:7–10
6.	The disappearance of heaven and earth and the second resurrection	20:11–15
7.	The new creation and God's eternal age	21:1–8
Epilogue	The New Jerusalem	21: 9–22: 21
	External appearance of the city	21:9–14
	Measurement of the city	21:15–17
	Composition of the city	21:18–21
	Divine glory of the city	21:22–27
	New Garden of Eden with the river and the Tree of Life	22:1–7
	John's concluding words	22:8–21

A Coded Scenario

The eagle chick fled from her mother's nest because her life was threatened as long as she remained. The mother sought the chick's return and, when she wouldn't return, decided to establish residence with the chick in order to retain control over her.

The eagle chick grew strong and developed to the point where she was self-sufficient and no longer needed the protection of her mother eagle. Mother wouldn't let go without a struggle. The little eagle had to fight and struggle in order to prove that she was capable of taking care of herself.

The little eagle grew into a beautiful young adult eagle and eventually met another eagle with which she mated. Over a period of time, one by one thirteen eggs were hatched and a brood of baby eagles began to establish themselves in their new home. Grandmother eagle was impressed with her grandchildren and wanted even more to have influence over them.

The grandchildren were respectful of grandmother eagle and tried to convince her that their first loyalty was to their mother, even if it meant causing their grandmother to be unhappy. In their unity they found strength and were able withstand all of the efforts of the grandmother when she tried to entice and persuade one or another of them to leave their mother to return to the flock of the grandmother.

The story continues through many more generations of birth and death and new life in the new land of the eagles.

The Seven Churches

A. Each individual or small group will work with one church and its corresponding passage.

1. Ephesus 2:1–7
2. Smyrna 2:8–11
3. Pergamum 2:12–17
4. Thyatira 2:18–27
5. Sardis 3:1–6
6. Philadelphia 3:7–13
7. Laodicea 3:14–22

B. Look for five things:

1. "These are the words of . . ." (a description of Christ)
2. "I know . . ." (words of commendation)
3. "I hold this against you . . ." (words of judgment)
4. "Remember . . . beware . . . repent . . . hold fast . . ." (words of admonition)
5. "He who conquers . . ." (words of hope and promise)

All Things New

Directions: Each person in the group will work with one of the following passages. Work individually or with another person or two. Read the passage and then answer the three questions below. Be prepared to share with the whole group some insights regarding your passage.

The following passages all speak of "something new":

1. Psalm 96:1–6 — "Sing to the LORD a new song"
2. Isaiah 43:14–21 — "I am about to do a new thing"
3. Isaiah 65:17–25 — "New heavens and a new earth"
4. Jeremiah 31:31–34 — "I will make a new covenant"
5. Luke 5:36–39 — The parable of the New Garment and the New Wineskin
6. Luke 22:14–20 — "This cup . . . is the new covenant"
7. 2 Corinthians 5:16–21 — Those in Christ are "a new creation"

Consider the following questions as you read one of the above passages:

1. What do you sense to be the context or the setting in which this emphasis on something new is to be understood?

2. What is the source of, or the reason for, the new?

3. What might be an expected result from the new?

Appendix

Various Bible Translations

New Revised Standard Version (NRSV)

The National Council of the Churches of Christ in the USA published the NRSV in 1990. The NRSV is the result of the work of thirty Bible scholars and attempts to reproduce the modern English equivalent of the original Hebrew and Greek words. This is the translation of choice for many educational publications and seminaries of the mainline denominations. A feature of the NRSV is its rendering of gender language as inclusive of men and women when the text implies that the intent of the writers was to be inclusive. The NRSV is a revision of the Revised Standard Version (RSV), published in 1952.

New International Version (NIV)

The NIV was published by the International Bible Society in 1978. The translation is the work of 115 Bible scholars from various countries and attempts to reproduce the modern English equivalent of the original Hebrew and Greek words. This is the translation of choice for many evangelical churches and curriculum writers.

Contemporary English Version (CEV)

The CEV was published by the American Bible Society in 1995. It is the work of more than one hundred translators and reviewers. This translation seeks to present a dynamic equivalent of the original languages by reproducing the meaning of the text in a contemporary, common language that can be understood by young Christians. A feature of the CEV is to render gender language as inclusive of men and women when the text implies that the intent of the writers was to be inclusive.

Today's English Version (TEV)

The TEV was published by the American Bible Society in 1976 and was first known as the Good News Bible. The primary translator of the New Testament was Robert Bratcher, who was joined by six other translators for the Old Testament. This is one of the first efforts to translate the Bible in the contemporary, common language of the readers. The TEV has been a favorite of children and youth and their teachers. One of the features of this translation is the use of line drawings by Annie Vallotton to illustrate various passages.

New King James Version (NKJV)

The NKJV was published in 1982 by Thomas Nelson Publishers and is the work of more than one hundred Bible scholars and translators. The NKJV is a revision of the original King James Version that was the major Bible in English for over three hundred years. The NKJV seeks to reproduce a contemporary English equivalent of the original Hebrew and Greek words and at the same time maintain the style of the original KJV.

Living Bible (LB)

The LB was published in 1971 by Tyndale Publishers and quickly became a best-seller. The LB is not a translation but a paraphrase of the American Standard Version (1901) by one man, Kenneth Taylor, who first started rendering the biblical text in a language and style that his children would understand. Taylor's goal was to "simplify the complex words of the Bible" and to do so from a "rigid evangelical position." One must not depend on a paraphrase, however, as the only source for in-depth Bible study.

An excellent resource for gaining more information about all of the above translations, and many more, is The Bible in English Translation: An Essential Guide, *by Steven M. Sheeley and Robert N. Nash Jr., published by Abingdon Press.*

Study Bibles

The Access Bible (NRSV). Oxford University Press, 1999. 1,753 pages.

Features of *The Access Bible* include introductory articles for each book of the Bible; sidebar essays, maps, and charts in places appropriate to the text; section-by-section commentaries on the text; a glossary; a brief concordance; and a section of Bible maps in color.

HarperCollins Study Bible (NRSV). HarperCollins Publishers in consultation with the Society of Biblical Literature, 1993. 2,346 pages.

Features of the *HarperCollins Study Bible* include introductory articles for each of the books of the Bible; extensive notes on the biblical text at the bottom of each page; inclusion of the Apocryphal/Deuterocanonical Books; maps within the text as well as a collection of maps in color in the back of the Bible; and a chart of quotations of the Jewish Scriptures in the New Testament.

The NIV Study Bible (NIV). Zondervan, 1985. 2,148 pages.

Features of the *NIV Study Bible* include introductory articles and outlines for each book of the Bible; extensive notes for explanation and interpretation of the biblical text on each page; helpful charts, maps, and diagrams within the biblical text; an index to subjects; a concise concordance; and a collection of maps in color.

The Learning Bible (CEV). American Bible Society, 2000. 2,391 pages.

Features of *The Learning Bible* include introductory articles and outlines for each book of the Bible; fifteen background articles and over one hundred miniarticles; charts and timelines; a miniatlas; notes on biblical texts in six categories, each identified by a different color and symbol (geography; people and nations; objects, plants, and animals; ideas and concepts; history and culture; and cross-references); and hundreds of illustrations, photographs, and diagrams in color.

The New Oxford Annotated Bible (NRSV), *Third Edition.* Oxford University Press, 2001. 2,398 pages.

Features of *The New Oxford Annotated Bible* include introductory articles for each book of the Bible; a number of maps and diagrams within the text; a series of essays on canons of the Bible, translation of the Bible in English, methods of interpretation, and cultural contexts; an index to topics included in the study notes; a brief concordance; and a section of Bible maps in color.

Bible Study Resources

The Concise Concordance of the New Revised Standard Version. John R. Kohlengerger III, editor. Oxford University Press, 1993.

Eerdmans' Handbook of the Bible. David Alexander and Pat Alexander. Lion Publishing, 1973.

Hammond's Atlas of the Bible Lands. Harry Thomas Frank, editor. Hammond, 1984.

Harper's Bible Commentary. James L. Mays, general editor with the Society of Biblical Literature. Harper & Row Publishers, 1988.

Harper's Bible Dictionary. Paul J. Achtemeier, general editor with the Society of Biblical Literature. Harper & Row Publishers, 1985.

The Lion Encyclopedia of the Bible. Pat Alexander, organizing editor. Lion Publishing, 1978.

Nelson's Complete Book of Bible Maps and Charts. Thomas Nelson Publishers, 1996.

Nelson's 3-D Bible Mapbook. Simon Jenkins. Thomas Nelson Publishers, 1985.

www.ingramcontent.com/pod-product-compliance
Lightning Source LLC
Chambersburg PA
CBHW080209230526
45370CB00003B/16
* 9 7 8 0 6 6 4 2 2 5 7 7 3 *